KNOWLEDGE REVIEW

7

Improving the use of research in social care practice

Isabel Walter, Sandra Nutley, Janie Percy-Smith,
Di McNeish and Sarah Frost

SCIE

Social Care Institute for Excellence

Better knowledge for better practice

First published in Great Britain in June 2004 by the Social Care Institute for
Excellence (SCIE)

Social Care Institute for Excellence
1st Floor
Goldings House
2 Hay's Lane
London SE1 2HB
UK
www.scie.org.uk

British Library Cataloguing in Publication Data

A catalogue record for this book is available from the British Library

ISBN 1 904812 13 9

Dr Isabel Walter is Senior Research Fellow and **Sandra Nutley** is Professor of
Public Policy and Management, and Director, both at the Research Unit for
Research Utilisation, Centre for Public Policy and Management, School of
Management, University of St Andrews. **Janie Percy-Smith** is a freelance
researcher/Visiting Professor at Leeds Metropolitan University. **Di McNeish** is
Director of Policy and Research, Barnardo's. **Sarah Frost** is a Development
Officer, 'What Works for Children?' project, ESRC Evidence Network/Policy and
Research Unit, Barnardo's.

Produced by The Policy Press
University of Bristol
Fourth Floor, Beacon House
Queen's Road
Bristol BS8 1QU
UK
www.policypress.org.uk

Front cover: photograph supplied by kind permission of www.JohnBirdsall.co.uk
Printed and bound in Great Britain by Hobbs the Printers Ltd, Southampton.

Contents

Preface

Evidence-informed policy and practice demands increasing recourse to research as a key source of knowledge about how to improve practice. However, there is little point in simply turning up the rate at which research flows to the social care workforce – little research in fact has direct applicability, many practitioners are not equipped to digest research, and appropriate support systems are lacking. What we need is a better understanding of the relationship between social care research and the work of social care practitioners, including what organisational structures are needed to realise the aim of using research to improve practice.

We are grateful to the authors for undertaking this review, which is the first of its kind to examine research use across the social care workforce as a whole. The review considers the use of research knowledge by social care staff and how research use can be promoted in social care practice. It examines evidence about effective ways of promoting research use in social care; explores models of research use that can include staff at different levels and settings in social care, and also organisational structures that support the use of research. A range of models embodying different ways of thinking about and developing the use of research in social care are explored, as well future directions for research and development in this area.

Most importantly, the review highlights evidence of a commitment to and belief in the importance of research for improving social care practice, despite the challenges this poses for the field of social care. In addition to its broad role in informing the debate about the use of research-based knowledge in social care, the review provides important pointers to underpin the work of the Social Care Institute for Excellence (SCIE) in promoting useful and relevant knowledge that will help to make a difference.

Wendy Hardyman
Research Analyst

Acknowledgements

The authors would like to acknowledge the help and support provided by other individuals within both the Research Unit for Research Utilisation (RURU) and Barnardo's. Within RURU this includes: Liz Brodie, who provided administrative support; Huw Davies, who provided comments on the literature review protocol and the final report; Jennifer Morton, who assisted with literature searching and cataloguing; and Joyce Wilkinson, who assisted with the independent checks on selecting, handling and quality assessing studies. Within Barnardo's this includes: Larraine Brown, Joanne Carson and Angela Jacobs who provided administrative support in organising the seminars; Julie Healy, Angela Hutton, Cathy McMahon, Helen Mills and Jo Stephens who took notes of the discussions at the seminars; and Angela Cooper, who transcribed the interviews undertaken.

For their time and contribution to this work, the authors would also like to thank all those participants who attended and took part in the four consultation seminars and those individuals in national agencies who agreed to be interviewed.

We would also like to thank our advisory group for their guidance and comments:

- Celia Atherton, Research in Practice (RiP)
- Annette Boaz, Economic and Social Research Council (ESRC) UK Centre for Evidence-based Policy and Practice, Queen Mary, University of London
- Mike Campbell, freelance consultant
- Carol Joughlin, freelance consultant
- Joan Orme, Department of Social Policy and Social Work, University of Glasgow

and the Social Care Institute for Excellence (SCIE) for their guidance throughout the review.

Glossary of terms and abbreviations

This section provides an introduction to the key terms and abbreviations used within the review.

Referencing findings and sources

The review draws on findings from two main sources:

- 28 empirical studies reported in the literature on research utilisation in social care;
- fieldwork conducted by members of the review team, which involved seminars with social care staff and representatives from service user organisations and interviews with key personnel in the social care field.

Thirty-seven empirical studies initially selected as relevant from the literature were quality assessed (see Appendices 1 and 4). As a result, we divided studies into:

- category A: good quality studies (14 studies);
- category B: less robust studies (14 studies);
- category C: studies whose quality could not be established to be adequate (9 studies). Findings from these nine studies were excluded from the review.

Within the review, findings from the 28 category A and B studies are referenced as (**A1**, **A2**), (**B1**, **B2**) and so on. It should be noted that sometimes the same study was reported in more than one paper, and in one instance different findings from the same study are reported in two different papers. Thus, studies do not always correspond to individual papers. An annotated bibliography of all 37 quality assessed studies is given in Appendix 5.

Findings from the fieldwork seminars and interviews are referenced as (**S/I**).

Individual papers are referenced numerically ([1,2,3] and so on).

Examples of research utilisation initiatives within documents provided by Social Services Departments are referenced as (**SSD**).

Types of knowledge

Research utilisation in social care involves integrating knowledge from research with other forms of knowledge, such as knowledge from practice experience. There is a substantial literature on the nature of knowledge, and it was beyond the remit of this review to explore this field in any depth. For the purposes of the review, we have used a framework for understanding knowledge provided by another SCIE report, *Types and quality of knowledge in social care*[1]. This sets out a classification of knowledge in social care as follows:

1. *Organisational knowledge:* knowledge gained from organising social care, through governance and regulation activities.
2. *Practitioner knowledge:* knowledge gained from doing social care, which tends to be tacit, personal and context-specific.
3. *User knowledge:* knowledge gained from experience of and reflection on using social care services, which again is often tacit. Within this review user knowledge is termed service user knowledge.
4. *Research knowledge:* knowledge gathered systematically within a planned strategy, which is mostly explicit and provided in reports, evaluations and so forth. In this review, evidence is defined as empirical findings from research.
5. *Policy community knowledge*: knowledge gained from the wider policy context and residing in the civil service, ministries, think tanks and agencies.

The review was concerned with the ways in which research knowledge is utilised within social care, which in turn involves interaction and integration with other forms of knowledge.

Key terms

Key terms used in the report are listed alphabetically below. When one of these terms is used for the first time in the review, it appears in purple.

(A1, A2)   A reference to findings from good quality studies located in the literature.

(B1, B2)   A reference to findings from less robust studies located in the literature.

(C1, C2)   This refers to studies whose findings were not judged to be sufficiently robust and which were excluded from the empirical data synthesis of the review.

CEBSS   The Centre for Evidence-based Social Services (CEBSS) was set up in 1997 and is a partnership between the Department of Health, a consortium of Social Services Departments (SSDs) in the South West of England and the University of Exeter. Its main aim is to ensure that decisions taken at all levels within social services are informed by good quality research. CEBSS' member organisations receive support, training and advice on meeting this broad aim.

Empirical   Empirical means derived from observation or experiment. In this review, empirical studies were defined as research studies that report clear outcome data. These data may have been qualitative or quantitative in form. Empirical papers were those that reported findings from empirical studies.

Evidence   Evidence is used to refer to empirical findings from research studies.

GSCC   The General Social Care Council (GSCC) is responsible for regulating the social care workforce and for promoting high standards of practice and training in social care in England. Similar Care

	Councils have also been established in Northern Ireland and Wales.
HRM	Human resource management (HRM); it refers to the ideas and practices for the management of people at work.
Human services	The term human services is used to refer to staff working in social care settings within North America to reflect differences in terms used by social workers and academics there.
ICCR	Institute of Child Care Research at Queen's University, Belfast. The Institute aims to play a key role in influencing the development of child care policy and practice in Northern Ireland through undertaking original research and providing training and consultation on conducting and using research.
Inductive analysis	An inductive analysis begins with observations in order to develop broader understandings, instead of starting with established theories to explain those observations. It argues from the particular to the general.
Making Research Count	This is a collaborative venture between ten English universities that offers staff in local authority SSDs and other agencies working jointly with these departments the opportunity to work in partnership with academic colleagues to develop evidence-based social work and social care practice, and to improve the dissemination of research. It aims to ensure that operational staff are involved in setting the research agenda, and that both they and service users benefit from the outcomes. The scheme offers members seminars and workshops to support research literacy and to equip them with evaluation expertise. A subscribing authority is linked to one of the ten universities, normally the nearest. Authorities within a regional grouping will meet to share news and views and plan activities.

NCSC	The National Care Standards Commission (NCSC) is responsible for ensuring that care services in England meet national minimum standards determined by the Secretary of State for Health. From 1 April 2004 the NCSC was replaced by the Commission for Social Care Inspection (CSCI) which brings together the NCSC with the Social Services Inspectorate (SSI).
Organisational knowledge	Knowledge gained from organising social care. See 'Types of knowledge', above.
Policy community knowledge	Knowledge gained from the wider policy context. See 'Types of knowledge', above.
Practice managers	We use the term 'practice managers' as a generic term for managers working in service delivery organisations. When we wish to distinguish between different levels of management we have used terms such as 'senior managers' and 'team managers'.
Practitioner knowledge	Knowledge gained from doing social care. See 'Types of knowledge', above.
Qualitative	Qualitative research methods aim to understand the dynamics of social phenomena in their natural context, and to generate rich description from diverse perspectives. They produce data in different forms but typically as language. In this review, qualitative methods used in studies mainly involved interviews and group discussions.
Quantitative	Quantitative research methods aim to measure or quantitatively assess social phenomena; to describe representative samples in quantitative terms; and to estimate or test quantitative relationships. They produce data in numeric form. In this review, quantitative methods used in studies mainly involved questionnaire surveys.

Research	Research comprises the results from systematic investigations based on planned research strategies. This may be primary research that involves systematic inquiry based on observation or experiment. It may also be secondary research, research that takes primary research studies as its objects of inquiry. When looking at studies of the utilisation of research, however, we often had to rely on what the original authors took to mean research. In some cases this represented study respondents' own definitions of research. It was rare for the research utilisation studies we examined to set out clear definitions of research. We did not examine the use of other forms of information, such as performance management data. This is better defined as **organisational knowledge** (see above).
Research knowledge	Knowledge derived from research. See 'Types of knowledge', above.
Research-based practitioner	We use the term 'research-based practitioner' to define one of our three models of research use in social care to distinguish this model from more general use of the term 'research-informed practitioner'.
Research-informed practice	Throughout the review, we use the term 'research-informed practice', rather than 'research-based practice'. This recognises the diverse and often subtle ways in which research can impact on practice, and the fact that there are other influences on practice.
Research use/ research utilisation	Research use refers to a wide range of impacts that research may have on policy and practice. Research use need not only mean that research has a direct impact on decision making. It can also include raising awareness of research findings; changing attitudes and beliefs; and increasing knowledge and understanding (Chapter 2, page 9).

Research in Practice

Research in Practice (RiP) is a partnership between the Dartington Hall Trust, the Association of Directors of Social Services and the University of Sheffield, with over 75 participating English local authorities, voluntary child care organisations, Local Strategic Partnerships (LSPs) and Primary Care Trusts (PCTs). It aims to promote the use of evidence to improve experiences and outcomes for vulnerable children and families, and the capacity of policy, services and professionals to respond to the needs of these. It does so by working closely with member agencies to test new methods of promoting the use of evidence, and by promoting the use of evidence through professional development and other services.

Research Unit for Research Utilisation

The Research Unit for Research Utilisation (RURU), based at the University of St Andrews, is a member of the ESRC's UK Network for Evidence-based Policy and Practice. The overall aim of the Unit is to facilitate the production and use of practical knowledge that will assist in enhancing the role of research in public policy and public services. Its role is to develop a resource concerned with the use of research across the health, criminal justice, education and social care sectors. As part of this resource, the Unit has developed a database of papers relevant to research use in these fields.

Social Care Institute for Excellence

The Social Care Institute for Excellence (SCIE) gathers and publicises knowledge about how to make social care services better. SCIE is an independent organisation created in response to the government drive to improve quality in social care services across England and Wales. It was launched in October 2001. SCIE is funded by the Department of Health and the Welsh Assembly. SCIE will be working with the Northern Ireland Assembly in the future, and already has links with the Scottish Executive.

Service user knowledge
: Knowledge gained from experience of and reflection on service use. See 'Types of knowledge', above.

(S/I)
: Refers to findings from the fieldwork seminars and interviews conducted for this review.

Social care
: Within the review, social care refers to the full range of services provided across different social care settings within the UK. This covers a wide range of areas, including home care, day care and residential care for older people; fieldwork with young people and families; residential care and fostering for children; and supporting people with physical disabilities, learning disabilities and mental health problems in residential care and in their homes. It also includes both the professionally qualified workforce and staff without professional qualifications. However, it excludes probation services.

Social workers
: Where findings from studies are reported, we have tried to reflect authors' descriptions of study participants. Social workers generally refers to staff with professional social work qualifications. Professional social care staff includes staff working in social care settings with professional qualifications that need not be social work qualifications. Social care staff includes any staff working in social care settings.

SSD
: Social Services Department.

(SSD)
: Refers to examples from documents provided by SSDs for this review.

Practice tools
: In this review, we have used the term 'practice tools' to refer to practical products that have been developed using research findings. These include paper-based tools such as practice checklists and outcome or risk assessment forms. They also

include formats such as wall charts or reminder cards.

Topss England   The Training Organisation for Personal Social Services (Topss England) is responsible for training needs analysis, a national training strategy, workforce planning, national occupational standards, and the national qualifications framework for social care in England. In Northern Ireland and Wales, the functions of Topss are undertaken by respective Social Care Councils.

Users   Throughout this review, we have used the term 'user' to refer to users of research. We are aware that this term is more regularly used within the social care field to refer to users of social care services. For clarity, we refer to the latter group as 'service users'.

Whole systems approach   A whole systems approach is a way of thinking which suggests that to understand an area of practice, we need to look at more than single individuals or single organisations acting in isolation. Instead, we need to examine the interconnections and relationships between different people and organisations, and any potential synergy or conflicts between them, within the whole social care system. A systems approach assumes that the system will work best if all parts of the system work together in complementary ways.

Summary

The aim of this knowledge review was to understand how social care staff use research knowledge and how research use can be promoted in the sector. It had five main objectives:

- to examine how research is used in social care;
- to review the evidence about the effectiveness of different ways of promoting the use of research in social care;
- to consider models of research use that can include staff at all levels and all settings in social care;
- to provide an overview of models of learning and human resource management (HRM) that support the use of research;
- to analyse future directions for research and development in research use and practice change in social care.

The review was undertaken through systematic search and analysis of the literature, supported by fieldwork seminars and interviews. Over 3,000 papers were identified and sifted using selection criteria. A total of 191 were selected as relevant to the review. Most of these contained conceptual discussion or described examples of initiatives to promote the use of research. Evidence on the use of research and on the effectiveness of initiatives to promote research use came from 28 quality assessed studies. This evidence was supplemented by findings from four consultation seminars with 135 social care practitioners and educators, and from seven interviews with senior personnel in the field. Relevant documents were also obtained from social services departments (SSDs).

A wide range of applications for research are reported, and these may be both direct – developing policy and practice – and indirect – using research to provide knowledge and new ideas. The picture that emerges is of pockets of research-aware individuals who may be found at any level within an organisation, although research appears to be more distant from the practice concerns of those in the independent care sector. Overall, there is evidence of a commitment to and belief in the importance of research for improving social care practice, reflected in a wide range of activities to promote research use.

Analysis of current practice produced three different models that embody different ways of thinking about and developing the use of research in social care:

The research-based practitioner model:

- it is the role and responsibility of the individual practitioner to keep up to date with research and apply it to practice;
- the use of research is a linear process;
- practitioners have high levels of professional autonomy to change practice based on research;
- professional education and training are important in enabling research use.

Findings suggest that the successful development of this model faces a number of barriers in terms of capacity to access and interpret research. These barriers are being addressed but there is limited evidence about the effectiveness of such initiatives.

The embedded research model:

- research–informed practice is achieved by embedding research in the systems and processes of social care, such as standards, policies, procedures and tools;
- responsibility for ensuring research-informed practice lies with policy makers and service delivery managers;
- the use of research is a linear and instrumental process;
- funding restrictions, performance management, inspection and appraisal regimes are used to encourage research-informed practice.

There is little evidence about the success of this model that remains relatively undeveloped within the UK social care sector.

The organisational excellence model:

- the key to successful research use lies with social care delivery organisations: their leadership, management and organisation;
- research use is supported by developing a research-minded culture;
- there is local adaptation of research findings and ongoing learning within organisations;

- partnerships with local universities and intermediary organisations facilitate the creation and use of research.

The review found support for this model among members of the social care workforce, but limited evidence of its effectiveness in practice.

The three models are not mutually exclusive. A whole systems approach to thinking about the use of research in social care identified the extent to which the models complement one another.

Key tensions emerge around:

- different levels of autonomy in applying the findings from research;
- linear adoption of findings versus a collaborative approach to the creation and use of research knowledge.

Key gaps are:

- the need to engage research funders;
- lack of a core role for service users in supporting the use of research.

Different models may also be more relevant for different sections of the social care workforce, at different stages of developing research use initiatives and for different types of research.

Four key conclusions emerge from the review:

- there is much activity to promote research use in social care, but this needs to be coordinated to avoid duplication and ensure best practice is shared;
- the diversity of the social care field, in terms of service delivery organisations, client groups and workforce, demands a variety of actions to promote use. Such actions also need to take into account multiagency and multidisciplinary working;
- robust evidence of what works in promoting research use in social care is limited, and tends to focus on the professionally qualified workforce;
- a whole systems approach for enhancing research use in social care may be a positive way forward.

Whole systems development would have significant implications for approaches to learning and HRM in social care, which needs to be multifaceted and applied flexibly.

Future research and development on research use needs to attend to:

- the non-professional workforce, and the use of research at organisational and system levels;
- use of research within the embedded research model;
- evaluating initiatives that aim to promote research use;
- the integration of different types of knowledge in using research;
- how research use is best defined and measured.

There are three main recommendations:

- the social care field should use this review as a starting point to take stock of current initiatives to promote research use;
- a whole systems approach offers a useful framework for promoting and developing research use in social care;
- a research and development agenda needs to be articulated and pursued in order to ensure initiatives to promote research use are themselves based on good evidence.

List of acronyms

BPG	Best Practice Guide
CASP	Critical Appraisal Skills Programme
CEBSS	Centre for Evidence-based Social Services
CoP	Communities of Practice
CSCI	Commission for Social Care Inspection
DHSS	Department of Health and Social Services
DSRU	Dartington Social Research Unit
EBM	evidence-based medicine
eLSC	Electronic Library for Social Care
ESO	Environment Scanning Overview
ESRC	Economic and Social Research Council
GSCC	General Social Care Council
HRM	human resource management
ICCR	Institute of Child Care Research
JRF	Joseph Rowntree Foundation
LGA	Local Government Association
LGRU	Local and Regional Government Research Unit
LSPs	Local Strategic Plans
MRC	Making Research Count
NCDDR	National Center for the Dissemination of Disability Research
NCSC	National Care Standards Commission
ODPM	Office of the Deputy Prime Minister
OPM	Office for Public Management
PCG	Primary Care Group
PCT	Primary Care Trust
RCT	randomised controlled trial
RiP	Research in Practice
RURU	Research Unit for Research Utilisation
SCIE	Social Care Institute for Excellence
SSD	Social Services Department
SSI	Social Services Inspectorate
Topss	Training Organisation for Personal Social Services
UKHCA	UK Home Care Association
WWFC	'What Works for Children'

1

Introduction

Getting social care staff to use research knowledge in their day-to-day work is a key aspect of the drive to modernise social care. As part of this drive, the role of the Social Care Institute for Excellence (SCIE) is to gather and publicise knowledge of what works in social care. Yet there is a lack of understanding in the field about whether and how staff use the fruits of research. The aim of this review is to understand how social care staff use research knowledge and how research use can be promoted and enhanced.

The review has five main objectives:

- to examine how research is used in social care;
- to review evidence about the effectiveness of different ways of promoting the use of research in social care;
- to consider models of research use that can include staff at all levels and in all settings in social care;
- to provide an overview of models of learning and human resource management (HRM) that support the use of research;
- to analyse future directions for research and development in research use and practice change in social care.

The review aimed to cover the use of research across different social care settings within the UK. It was not restricted to the professionally qualified workforce and its scope included a wide range of jobs: home care and residential care for older people, supporting children, young people and families, and assisting people with physical disabilities, learning disabilities and mental health problems. Probation services were excluded. In practice the review covers a more limited range of settings and workforce that reflects the nature of the literature in this field.

Questions about what counts as evidence and knowledge in social care are important to debates about the use of research in the sector. This issue has, however, been considered by other work commissioned by SCIE[1], and is beyond the scope of this review.

The review was undertaken by a team that drew on the complementary experience and expertise of two organisations:

- the Research Unit for Research Utilisation (RURU) at the University of St Andrews;
- Barnardo's Research and Development Team.

The team received guidance and comments from an advisory group comprising:

- Celia Atherton, Research in Practice (RiP)
- Annette Boaz, Economic and Social Research Council (ESRC) UK Centre for Evidence-based Policy and Practice, Queen Mary, University of London
- Mike Campbell, freelance consultant
- Carol Joughlin, freelance consultant
- Joan Orme, Department of Social Policy and Social Work, University of Glasgow.

Guidance on the review was also provided by SCIE.

In undertaking the review, a systematic search and examination of documented studies and current thinking on research use in social care was supplemented by fieldwork seminars and interviews to help address gaps in the literature and capture emerging knowledge.

The findings from the literature review and the fieldwork were catalogued separately and then synthesised thematically. This analysis led to the development of three models of research use within social care. The assumptions underpinning each of these models, the activities associated with them, and the extent to which there is evidence to support their effectiveness, was explored.

The synergies and tensions between the three models were identified in the process of developing a whole systems approach to understanding and promoting research use in social care. This analysis resulted in a set of recommendations for the social care field, including the implications for HRM and learning and the requirements of future research and development work on research use.

This work is reported in the four chapters that follow. Chapter 2 summarises the methods and findings of the literature review, seminars and interviews. Chapter 3 presents three emerging models of research use in social care. Chapter 4 outlines a whole systems approach to understanding and promoting research use in social care. Chapter 5 concludes the review and details main recommendations.

2

Review methods and findings

In this chapter, the review methods are summarised and the main findings and themes to emerge from the literature review and the fieldwork seminars and interviews are reported.

The main findings from the literature review and fieldwork were captured by four key questions:

- How is research used in social care?
- How is research use promoted in social care?
- How effective are different methods of promoting research use?
- What are the barriers and enablers to research use in social care?

This chapter reports the findings relating to the first two questions. Discussion of these findings is developed further in Chapter 3, where evidence on the effectiveness of different methods of promoting research use and the barriers and enablers they face are also reported.

2.1. The literature review

The literature review took a systematic approach to searching the literature, selecting papers for inclusion and extracting data from papers, and to quality assessing empirical studies. A wide range of databases and websites were searched, and some papers were also identified through personal contacts. Over 3,000 references were retrieved and these were sifted using defined selection criteria. A total of 191 papers were finally selected as relevant to the review[2-192]. A full description of methods is provided in Appendix 1. The database search strategy is provided in Appendix 6.

Key data were extracted from the 191 papers selected for the review and form the basis for a map of this literature. Seventy-five per cent of the papers are journal articles, and 10% are published reports. The remainder are books and book chapters, online reports and conference papers. Over half of the 191 papers date from 2000 or later.

Papers were categorised according to whether they:

* report findings from empirical studies: empirical papers (*n*=62)
4, 8-9, 13-15, 20, 23, 30, 33, 35, 37, 40, 43-44, 46, 55, 61, 66, 70, 72-3, 82, 84-5, 93, 99, 105, 108-9, 115, 119, 121-3, 125, 127-30, 135, 140-1, 144, 146, 151, 154-5, 157-61, 164, 168, 170, 172, 177, 182, 184, 188-9

* contain some conceptual discussion: conceptual papers (*n*=135)
3-6, 8-9, 11-12, 16, 18-20, 22-3, 26-9, 32, 35, 37-42, 44, 46-55, 57-61, 64-6, 68-72, 77-8, 81, 83-9, 91-2, 94-9, 101, 103-6, 111-14, 116-20, 122-5, 127-34, 136-40, 142, 146-9, 151-6, 159, 162, 165-7, 169-70, 173-88, 190, 192

* describe examples of initiatives to promote research use: example papers (*n*=56)
2, 7, 10, 12, 17-19, 21, 23-6, 29, 31, 34, 36-8, 45, 56, 62-3, 65, 67, 71, 74-6, 79-80, 86, 90, 93, 100, 102, 107, 110, 114, 121, 124-7, 132, 134, 137, 140, 143, 145, 149-50, 154, 163, 171, 188, 191

Some papers fitted more than one of these categories, such as papers reporting empirical studies that also contain some conceptual discussion. Appendix 1 gives further details about the selection criteria used to categorise papers in this way.

Sixty-two of the 191 papers report findings from empirical studies. Half of the studies they describe were conducted in the UK, and most of the remainder were conducted in North America. Two main types of study were identified:

* studies of the use of research by policy makers or practitioners;
* studies of initiatives to promote the use of research.

A more detailed map of the literature is provided in Appendix 2.

Resource and time constraints meant it was not feasible to extract data from and quality assess all the studies reported in the 62 empirical papers. A decision was therefore taken to examine in depth only those studies conducted within UK social care settings, including reviews of such studies. Two non-UK studies were, however, examined in depth because they explored a topic not covered by the UK studies. Appendix 1 gives further details about these decisions, and the flow chart outlines the process of study selection. This led to studies reported in 24 papers being excluded at this stage of the review[4, 9, 14-15, 20, 33, 35, 43, 55, 61, 73, 82, 84-5, 122, 123, 129, 146, 151, 157, 170, 182, 184, 189].

We extracted in-depth data from 37 studies in total (detailed in

Appendix 5). Each of these studies was quality assessed and designated as:

- category A: good quality (**A1–A14**)
- category B: less robust (**B1–B14**) or
- category C: not possible to establish adequate quality (**C1–C9**).

Empirical findings from studies designated category C were excluded from the review's findings. This meant that empirical findings from 28 studies in total were included in the review. Appendix 4 provides details of the quality assessment process.

In addition to papers retrieved from the literature review, a letter was sent to all UK Directors of Social Services (excluding Scotland) requesting copies of any relevant literature. Documents were received from 22 Social Services Departments (SSDs) in all. They were handled separately from other selected papers (see Appendix 1). None of these documents is directly cited in the review, but all were scanned for relevance.

2.2. Limitations of the literature

Two main points should be considered in reading the review:

- The effective delivery of social care means involving all stakeholders, including service users. However, we found that this latter group was largely absent from the social care literature about research utilisation. Our search strategy was inclusive and should have uncovered any evidence about the differential impact of research that involved or was led by service users. It should also have identified any initiatives to promote research use that involved this group. Some research and/or development work reported did include service users at different stages (for example, **A11**, **A12**), but it was not possible to discern the specific effect that service user involvement had on the impact of the research.
- Our searches retrieved a large number of papers containing in-depth conceptual discussion about the use of social research within social care and more generally. However, the focus of this review was on empirical findings. We do not report on the contents of the conceptual literature in any depth. Readers wishing to investigate this literature

further will find some pointers to key papers within the References section.

2.3. The fieldwork seminars and interviews

To supplement the literature review and capture emerging knowledge about research use, four consultation seminars and seven interviews were held with people in the social care field.

- The consultation seminars were held in Leeds, London, Belfast and Cardiff. They were attended by a total of 135 social care practitioners and educators from the voluntary and statutory sectors. In most cases those attending were managers rather than front-line workers. Following the seminars, information on specific research use initiatives were provided on request from individuals who attended the seminars.
- The interviews were with key personnel in the General Social Care Council (GSCC), Training Organisation for Personal Social Services (Topss England), National Care Homes Association, UK Home Care Association (UKHCA), Department of Health, Shaping Our Lives, and Wales Office of Research and Development.

The structure of the seminars and interviews and an analysis of those involved can be found in Appendix 3.

2.4. Synthesising the findings from the literature review and fieldwork elements

The literature review and fieldwork elements of the project provided both qualitative and quantitative findings. Quantitative data, typically from surveys, were too varied to allow useful quantitative aggregation. Further, it was not always clear that these results could be generalised to wider populations. Qualitative findings were often not presented in a conceptual form that could support established methods of synthesis of qualitative data, such as meta-ethnography. Because of this diversity we applied alternative approaches to synthesis, which aimed to be systematic.

Findings from the 28 studies included in the review and from the fieldwork were extracted and summarised according to six questions based on the review's main objectives (see Appendix 1). We then identified common themes or categories that occurred across these different sets of findings. Themes were developed independently for findings from category A and category B studies, but no theme was identified in findings from the less robust studies that had not already been identified within the better quality findings.

To develop models of research use in social care, we used an inductive analysis based on two sources of data:

- the themes identified by the review team;
- examples of activities to promote research use.

As a team, we analysed the different ideas and assumptions about research use in social care embedded within these sources to identify different models of the research use process. Using two or more researchers in this way in conducting qualitative analysis helps ensure the process is rigorous and that findings and conclusions are well grounded in the original data[193]. We then returned to the individual findings extracted from the literature and fieldwork to search for evidence about the likely effectiveness of the models. Where two or more studies reported similar evidence, their findings were collated using a traditional narrative approach to synthesis. A fuller account of the synthesis process is provided in Appendix 1.

2.5. How research is used in social care

How research is used and how research use is promoted are interrelated questions. For example, initiatives to promote research use may encourage particular forms of use and, conversely, the ways in which research is currently used are likely to influence the design of initiatives to increase this. Despite these interactions, the questions about research use and research use promotion are reported separately at this stage. The general use of research is considered here. Findings from studies that have evaluated and/or described particular initiatives to increase research use are discussed later.

Using research can mean many different things: raising awareness of research findings; challenging attitudes and perceptions; or changes in policy or practice or in outcomes for service users. The empirical studies whose findings were included in the review examined a range of different measures of research use, for example:

- reading research
- completing research-based assessment forms
- changes in knowledge
- the channels through which research gets disseminated
- perceptions of the value of interventions to promote research use
- outputs from research
- changes in practice or policy
- outcomes for service users.

Most often the measures used were subjective, as reported by study respondents. Further, it was rare for the use of research to be explicitly defined within these studies, although there were exceptions (for example, **B2**, **B14**). A few studies enabled respondents to define what the use of research meant for them, and our seminars and interviews took this approach. Given the diverse ways that studies assessed research use, it has not been possible to draw out findings from across studies about different kinds of research use. In reporting findings, we have had to rely on studies' own assessments of research use.

To consider how research is used in social care, the review analysed those studies that have asked social care staff about their general use of research. The analysis of these studies revealed two aspects to this issue: whether and how research is accessed, and how research is actually applied (that is, the purposes to which research is put). The findings on each of these aspects are presented in terms of the themes that emerged from our analysis across different studies and the seminars and interviews. We focus on themes because the nature of the evidence uncovered by the review means that it is not possible to provide robust quantitative findings answering questions such as how much, or how often, about these issues.

2.5.1. Research access

Given that much of the literature has focused on asking individuals within the social care field about how they access research, it is not surprising that a key theme to emerge from these studies is the importance of the individual (practitioner/manager/policy maker) in determining whether and how research is accessed. That is, the ways in which research is accessed and distributed appear to depend on individuals reading and circulating material, rather than groups of staff being introduced to research via other means such as staff development and training.

In so far as it happens, an individual's access to research may be both active – searching for relevant materials – and passive – disseminated materials landing on a desk (see below). Personal contact with peers and colleagues, and sometimes with researchers themselves, is important in understanding which research is accessed. When asked to comment on how they find out about research, individuals report that they access research as original findings rather than through reading about research in other documents, such as policy documents. However, individuals may not be aware that documents such as policy or guidance are research-based unless this research is referenced explicitly.

Sources/access to research findings

The following were detailed in several studies as the means by which research is accessed:

- department/agency circulation of research findings and briefings
- library facilities
- professional magazines*
- word of mouth
- personal links with researchers
- individual initiative/searching
- participation in workshops, seminars and conferences

Note: *Several studies refer to research being accessed via professional magazines such as *Community Care*. The interview with UKHCA indicated that the independent sector views *Community Care* as a "social service magazine". The *Caring Times* and *This Caring Business* are viewed as "independent sector magazines".

These themes have been identified from studies that have looked primarily at professionally qualified social care staff (including social care managers and other senior personnel). They comprise individuals working across a range of social care fields including mental health, adult services and children and families. It is difficult to discern patterns within these groups, and evidence about which groups are most likely to be aware of and use research appears contradictory (**B1; S/I**). Little evidence was unearthed about research use by social care staff without professional qualifications. In addition, interviews conducted with representatives of the independent sector suggest that research is often seen as distant from their concerns.

2.5.2. Research application

Studies of research use highlight that research can be applied both directly (for example, to develop policy and practice) and indirectly (for example, as a background to policy development or to support a political stance). However, within these categories there is a wide range of applications for research (see below).

Applications of research in social care

Self-report comments included in studies of research use indicate that research is used to:

- provide a foundation for restructuring services
- inform policy and practice reviews and development work
- address specific issues (problem solving)
- support a policy stance or argument
- promote reasoned debate
- assist with service monitoring and review
- provide quality assurance
- safeguard or justify funding

Comments in our seminars and interviews also indicate that research is sometimes used at a policy level to inform:

- care standards
- occupational standards
- educational and training requirements

In research use studies, policy uses of research are more likely to be reported than practice applications. This finding was echoed in the seminars, where participants offered very few examples of how research is actually used to inform practice. Documents received from SSDs provide indication of wide-ranging use of research in the development of policy, strategy and procedures, but also of ongoing activities that support the use of research in practice, such as staff and practice development and research-based training.

Given the disparate nature of studies included in the review, which rely largely on self-report data about research use, it is difficult to provide an overall assessment of the extent to which research informs policy and practice within social care. Further, individual respondents may be unaware of the extent to which policy documents or the training they receive are grounded in findings from research. The overall picture that emerges from the literature is of pockets of individually research-aware social care staff, who may be found at any level within an organisation.

Yet a theme that recurs throughout all the studies is of a commitment to and belief in the importance and value of research for improving social care practice. This was echoed in the seminars and interviews, and is reflected in the wide array of initiatives the review uncovered for promoting research use in social care.

2.6. How research use is promoted in social care

The overwhelming message to emerge from the literature review (including the large number of documents supplied by SSDs), seminars and interviews, is that there are a lot of people actively involved in many, wide-ranging activities aimed at increasing research use in social care.

In this section, these activities are grouped under seven main headings:

- ensuring a relevant research base;
- ensuring access to research;
- making research comprehensible;
- drawing out the practice implications of research;
- developing best practice models;
- requiring research-informed practice;
- developing a culture that supports research use.

These categories highlight the main purpose of various activities, but as many activities are multipurpose they may appear under several headings. In particular, researcher/research user networks and collaborations frequently have multiple objectives and may, indeed, be underpinned by the view that it is the activity itself (collaboration) that is important. Furthermore, the purposes served by such collaborations are likely to be dynamic rather than predetermined.

Within each of the seven categories of activity there is a variety of people and organisations engaged in promoting research use. Table 1 highlights some key activities currently being undertaken by six main groups of people/organisations:

- *governance organisations:* intermediaries whose secondary aims include the promotion and facilitation of research use (such as the Department of Health, Topss England);
- *research:* research organisations, research funders, research managers and individual researchers;
- *practice:* front-line practitioners, practice managers, practice-based intermediaries (such as local policy or research development officers);
- *training:* training and social work education organisations, trainers and educators, and human resource systems;
- *service users:* individual service users and their representative organisations;
- *facilitators,* whose primary purpose is the promotion and facilitation of research-informed practice (such as SCIE, RiP, whose focus is on children and families, and Making Research Count [MRC]).

It is notable from Table 1 that one set of stakeholders, service users, appear currently to play only a limited role in promoting the use of research.

Each category of activity is described in more detail below, including examples of a range of national and local initiatives.

Table 1: Summary of activities to promote research use by different people and organisations

Activities	People and organisations					
	Governance: organisations with secondary research use aims, eg Department of Health, Topss England	*Research:* research funders, research organisations and researchers	*Practice:* practice organisations, practice managers and practitioners, practice-based intermediaries	*Training:* training organisations and trainers, social work educators, human resource systems	*Service users:* service user organisations, service users	*Facilitators:* organisations whose prime purpose is research use, eg MRC, CEBSS, RiP
Ensuring relevant research	• Commissioning large-scale or national research • Commissioning research review	• Commissioning fresh research and reviews of research • Responding to invitations to tender • Undertaking research driven by priorities, local needs • Undertaking reviews of research • Supporting practice organisations to undertake research	• Participating in research • Undertaking research • Commissioning local research and evaluation		• Participating in research	• Undertaking reviews of research • Undertaking research to fill gaps • Supporting practice organisations to undertake research

Ensuring access to research	• Distributing research findings at a national level • Providing access to databases, libraries and IT systems	• Distributing research findings using various communication channels	• Locally distributing research findings • Providing access to libraries, databases and IT systems • Providing guides to searching for research • Providing dedicated study time	• Training in use of information services • Training in searching for research • Providing dedicated study time	• Distributing research findings, locally and more widely • Providing access to databases, libraries and inquiry services • Providing guides to searching for research
Making research comprehensible	• Publishing tailored research reviews and overviews • Publishing accessible research reports	• Commissioning and producing accessible research summaries • Producing targeted publications for different audiences • Acting as expert consultants	• Enabling discussion of research by making time and forums for discussion • Hosting conferences and seminars • Identifying experts and providing a gateway to expertise • Producing research summaries and overviews	• Critical appraisal skills training • Training in research skills and undertaking research	• Producing research summaries and overviews • Producing tailored publications and other products in different media • Providing critical appraisal training for research users • Providing a gateway to expertise

Drawing out the practice implications of research	• Developing national guidelines and protocols • Funding research/research user networks and collaborations	• Identifying practice implications in research papers • Participating in research/research user networks and collaborations • Conducting action research	• Developing local guidelines and protocols • Participating in research/research user networks and collaborations • Undertaking action research • Acting as local champions for research	• Development of evidence-based practice guides • Research-based training	• Participating in the development of local guidelines and protocols	• Developing general guidelines and protocols • Organising and participating in research/research user networks and collaborations
Developing best practice models	• Identifying and labelling best practice • Sharing best practice	• Participating in the development of demonstration projects	• Facilitating development and demonstration projects • Participating in development and demonstration projects	• Research-based training		• Participating in development and demonstration projects • Sharing best practice

Requiring research-informed practice	• Design of training regimes • Development of standards incorporating research use	• As part of supervision/appraisal processes		• Incorporating use or championing of research into job descriptions • Developing new research/practice intermediary posts • Encouraging the use of research in supervision and appraisal
Developing a culture that supports research use	• Inclusion in national policy statements	• Advocacy in professional journals • Participating in research/research user networks and collaborations	• Incorporation into local policy statements • Local role modelling • Development of strategies for promoting research-informed practice • Acting as local research champions	• Incorporating use or championing of research into job descriptions • Developing new research/practice intermediary posts • Incorporation into the curriculum of initial training and continuing professional development • Advocacy in professional journals • Provision of subscription organisations – enabling service organisations to sign up to evidence-based practice

2.6.1. Ensuring a relevant research base

A key theme to emerge from the literature review and seminars is that social care practitioners and managers feel that research is often producer-driven and distant from their own local needs. However, we also uncovered a wide range of ways in which different groups, including not only researchers but also those in practice contexts and in facilitating and intermediary roles, are engaged in developing a research base that can inform policy and practice in social care. This involves:

- commissioning research in specific areas or undertaking such commissioned research, at both local and national levels;
- undertaking syntheses of existing research or collating relevant findings;
- practitioners or managers undertaking fresh research relevant to local needs;
- involving social care staff in developing research plans; and
- involving social care staff at all stages of the research process, for example through partnerships with research teams or in action research projects.

Ensuring research is relevant

The Institute for Child Care Research (ICCR) at the Queen's University of Belfast aims to play a key role in influencing the development of child care policy and practice. A core programme of research is designed by the Strategy and Policy Group, which comprises child care policy top level officials from the Department of Health and Social Services (DHSS), the four senior child care managers from each of the four local Health and Social Services Boards, and representatives from the University. Each project within the core programme has a support group comprising experts and service users in the area who help with all stages of the research process, including formulation of research questions and advice on draft findings and on encouraging access to/use of the research.[74]

2.6.2. Ensuring access to research

Within practice contexts, a number of initiatives are being undertaken to ensure policy makers and practitioners have better practical access to research. These include enhanced library services, information alerting systems, improved Internet access and the provision of research databases. Improving access to research by potential users is a key feature of the remit of a number of social care research centres, such as the Social Policy Research Unit at the University of York. Intermediaries and facilitators such as the Department of Health, the Centre for Evidence-based Social Services (CEBSS) and RiP, as well as local research/information officers, also play a role in getting research to users. This includes circulating findings within or across organisations and providing tailored searches of the literature.

Improving access to research

North Yorkshire County Council's Social Services Directorate produces a regular Environment Scanning Overview (ESO) document. A senior officer systematically scans a range of information sources, principally the Internet, journals and briefings, for potentially relevant initiatives including research. New initiatives are recorded on the ESO document that is presented to the Directorate Management Group at its weekly meetings. An annotated version of the ESO listing actions is then e-mailed to relevant staff to raise awareness of the new information and how to respond (**S/I**).

CEBSS has published a guide for practitioners to help them search more effectively for research-based materials. The guide gives details about different sources of social care research and how to search them (**SSD**).

2.6.3. Making research comprehensible

Other activities to promote research use focus on ensuring that research can be readily understood by potential users. This often involves producing research in user-friendly formats, for example as summaries or by providing key messages. There are also initiatives to improve users' abilities to understand and interpret research, such as critical appraisal skills training, research discussion groups and programmes to support social care staff to undertake research themselves. Researchers also offer advice and expertise to help users interpret research.

Making research comprehensible

'What Works for Children?' (WWFC) is a joint initiative between Barnardo's, City University and the University of York and is part of the UK-wide 'Evidence Network' (www.evidencenetwork.org). WWFC's Development Officer works directly with practitioners and service planners in Children's Fund Programmes in Yorkshire to develop their ability to acquire research, assess research, adapt its format and ultimately apply it in decisions. WWFC has developed a range of resources to make it easier for service planners to find and use research. These include a series of *Evidence Nuggets*, summaries of research findings on particular interventions (**S/I**).

Journal clubs act as educational tools, providing a forum in which critical appraisal skills can be learned and practised. For example, in Islington SSD an area of work is identified through consultations with practitioners and managers. Relevant articles are mailed to around 100 interested staff and a group of 12-20 typically take part in discussing articles (**S/I**).

2.6.4. Drawing out the practice implications of research

Some activities go a step further than helping users access and understand research by defining the implications of research for day-to-day practice. This involves researchers working closely with practitioners or policy makers to identify how the findings of research may be applied, locally or nationally. Guidelines and protocols based on research have also been developed and associated training courses introduced.

Drawing out practice implications

The eLSC (Electronic Library for Social Care) has published two web-based Best Practice Guides (BPGs). The BPGs aim to provide examples of good practice and to enable users to develop practitioner knowledge and apply it effectively in their day-to-day work. They combine findings from research with the knowledge of service users, carers and practitioners. The electronic format allows users to move easily between research abstracts, practice examples and links to official government publications or local organisations providing services. The website is also searchable and provides opportunities for users to feed back views on form and content (see)[107].

2.6.5. Developing best practice models

Research has also been integrated directly with practice through the development of 'best practice' models. This has involved developing pilot or demonstration projects based on findings from research that are supported at local levels, for example through the provision of training and other resources.

Developing best practice models

The 'Matching Needs and Services' method, developed by the Dartington Social Research Unit (DSRU), is based on research but has been designed for those in agency settings to classify children referred for help according to their need. The results are then applied to the design of new interventions to meet the needs of children, and to implement and evaluate the new approaches. The method has been applied in 12 sites across Europe and North America that reflect a range of administrative arrangements[90].

2.6.6. Requiring research-informed practice

Rather than simply supporting research use, some initiatives require that individuals and organisations demonstrate research-informed practice. Explicit examples of this approach were found at the national level.

Requiring research-informed practice

The Department of Health's new *Requirements for social work training* embed the use of research knowledge as part of the *National occupational standards for social work*. This is outlined in Key Role 6:·

- Research, analyse, evaluate, and use current knowledge of best social work practice.
- Work within agreed standards of social work practice and ensure own professional development.
- Manage complex ethical issues, dilemmas and conflicts.
- Contribute to the promotion of best social work practice. (See www.dh.gov.uk/assetRoot/04/06/02/62/04060262.pdf) (**S/I**)

2.6.7. Developing a culture that supports research use

Alongside more direct strategies to promote the use of research in social care lie a range of initiatives with a wider aim to develop a 'research-minded' culture within the sector. These take diverse forms, from incorporating learning about research into the curriculum of social care training and staff development, to the inclusion of research use in national policy statements. At a local level, leadership and management practices play an important role in developing a culture that supports research-informed practice, as do research champions. Membership of facilitating organisations such as MRC and RiP also encourages this kind of cultural change.

Developing a research-minded culture

Research in Practice, whose focus is on children and families, has grown as a developmental network that works closely with a small number of agencies, experimenting and evaluating with them a range of approaches to integrating research and practice. It is based on a partnership of agencies, for which RiP staff view themselves as a resource rather than as the organisation itself. RiP aims to build the capacity of service organisations to develop a research and evaluative culture. The focus is on local adaptation of research, and RiP supports a range of development groups working towards strategic and practice advancements. RiP's work is more concerned with changing culture than structure, supporting organisations to become open to new thinking and able to promote and respond positively to change[7].

In summary, the review has revealed that, in so far as social care staff are aware of research, they access it in different ways and through different media. The use that is made of research is similarly varied, although policy uses of research are more likely to be reported than practice applications. The review has found little evidence about research use by the non-professionally qualified social care workforce. There is, however, a commitment to the idea of using research to improve social care policy and practice. The wide array of initiatives aimed at promoting research use is a testament to this. In this chapter these initiatives and activities have been described and exemplified. In the next chapter the ways in which they are underpinned and used to support different models of research use are explored.

Three models of research use in social care

Three broad ways of thinking about and developing research–informed practice were identified from our analysis of findings from the literature review, seminars and interviews. These different approaches are encapsulated in three models:

- the research–based practitioner model;
- the embedded research model;
- the organisational excellence model.

Three models of research use in social care

Research-based practitioner model
- It is the role and responsibility of the individual practitioner to keep abreast of research and ensure that it is used to inform day-to-day practice.
- The use of research is a linear process of accessing, appraising and applying research.
- Practitioners have high levels of professional autonomy to change practice based on research.
- Professional education and training are important in enabling research use.

Embedded research model
- Research use is achieved by embedding research in the systems and processes of social care, such as standards, policies, procedures and tools.
- Responsibility for ensuring research use lies with policy makers and service delivery managers.
- The use of research is both a linear and instrumental process: research is translated directly into practice change.

- Funding, performance management and regulatory regimes are used to encourage the use of research-based guidance and tools.

Organisational excellence model
- The key to successful research use rests with social care delivery organisations: their leadership, management and organisation.
- Research use is supported by developing an organisational culture that is 'research-minded'.
- There is local adaptation of research findings and ongoing learning within organisations.
- Partnerships with local universities and intermediary organisations are used to facilitate both the creation and use of research knowledge.

In this chapter, the three models are described in terms of their underpinning assumptions, the key activities associated with them, whether there are specific barriers to their development, and whether there is evidence to support their efficacy.

The three models encapsulate what is happening on the ground to promote research use in social care. They are derived from and describe current activities in the UK social care field (see Appendix 1). However, they inevitably represent a simplification of reality. We have constructed the models as ways of understanding the processes and relationships currently involved in promoting research use in social care. By outlining the models, we draw attention to the assumptions and ways of thinking that underpin different approaches to developing the use of research. Such approaches are not 'value-free', but contain particular ideas about what research-informed practice means and how it is best achieved. Our models help surface these often implicit ideas. They also highlight the implications of adopting any one approach to promoting the use of research: for example, who is viewed as responsible for this activity, and where funds and actions will be focused.

Although they build from current practice, the models are not reflected directly in how practitioners and practice managers talk about research use. Neither the seminars nor the interviews provided many explicit examples of the ways in which those involved in social care think about or model research use. There were many statements about the importance and value of research-informed practice but there was very little unpicking of what this might mean. Aspects of the different models are, however, sometimes evident, if not always explicit, within the research questions posed by the empirical studies included in the review.

In this chapter what we report is based is on empirical findings from the review. However, at the end of the chapter, we look briefly at the extent to which the empirical models we identify reflect discussions in the theoretical literature about how to develop research-informed social care delivery.

3.1. The research-based practitioner model

The key to this model is that it is seen as the role and responsibility of the individual practitioner to seek out and keep abreast of the latest research, which then informs his or her day-to-day practice and decision making. Professionals identify best practice for service users by integrating research knowledge with their own practitioner or 'craft' knowledge and with service users' preferences and views. Research knowledge is thus applied in combination with practitioner knowledge and service user knowledge to inform a particular decision. This model assumes that social care staff have relatively high levels of autonomy in conducting their day-to-day practice.

The model is underpinned by a linear view of research use: existing research findings are accessed and appraised by practitioners, and then applied to the specific problem in hand. The role of service users lies at the end stage of this process. Practitioners review options with service users, and make decisions in relation to service users' preferences alongside findings from research.

We identified a range of activities and strategies to promote research use that reflect this model. For example, organisations such as CEBSS and MRC have provided training to develop practitioners' critical appraisal skills for assessing the relevance and quality of research for making decisions. The production of 'user-friendly' research findings aimed at practitioners, such as the Joseph Rowntree Foundation (JRF) *Findings* series, is another example. Initial professional training is important in developing the research-based practitioner model, and the model is reflected in aspects of the new *Requirements for social work training* (see Chapter 2); and in the GSCC requirements for registration for social workers, which places responsibility for professional development (for example, through study and reading) on the individual.

However, findings from a number of studies, and from our own fieldwork, raise some questions for implementing this model within social care. Many studies report that social care staff more often view the development of research-informed practice as a joint responsibility between individual staff and departments, rather than the responsibility of the practitioner alone (for example, **A1, A2, A3**), a view reflected in our seminars. There is some evidence that social workers and other groups of professionally qualified social care staff are more likely to view this as a solely departmental responsibility than occupational therapists (**A1**).

Further, most social care staff do not appear to read research as a matter of routine, and even where such reading takes place, it is not necessarily perceived to have an impact on practice (**A1; B3**). Individuals also report that they lack access to research findings, although pockets of good practice were identified (**A1, A3, A4; B4, B5; S/I**). Barriers to reading and accessing research were cited as:

- limited circulation of materials within organisations;
- lack of search skills;
- poor publicity for information services;
- lack of time and competing priorities. (**A3, A4; B3, B4, B5, B9; S/I**).

Despite a wide range of initiatives aimed at improving access to research for social care staff (see Chapter 2), we found no studies that had yet formally evaluated the success of such initiatives.

Social care staff also report that much of the research they access is irrelevant to practice concerns, or is not 'user-friendly', and the sheer volume of research is also an issue (**A1, A4; B5, B6**). The following example provides some evidence that improving the relevance and presentation of research may be an effective approach.

Improving the presentation of research

Child protection: Messages from the research (popularly known as the 'Blue Book') is a Department of Health publication that provides an overview of findings and messages for practice from 20 key research studies in the child protection field. The Blue Book was disseminated through extensive circulation of free copies, together with a high profile ministerial launch and a series of regional one-day seminars.

A 300-strong survey conducted two-and-a-half years after the Blue Book's original distribution assessed the extent to which its contents were known about and used. Two thirds of respondents were managers, and one quarter front-line practitioners. The survey found that the Blue Book was widely known, and almost all respondents were able to identify ways in which the publication had contributed to their professional development. Over half claimed the contents had affected their own or local practice in some way. Respondents liked the layout, structure, language and content of the Blue Book. However, they also wanted both training based on the research, and guidance on implementing the findings (**A5**).

Professional social care staff report lack of expertise to interpret research (**A1**; **B4**, **B5**), a finding supported by poor performance in basic research understanding tests (**A1**). Some staff have suggested that research should come 'kite marked' for quality (**B5**; **S/I**). Critical appraisal skills training may also help address this barrier.

Critical appraisal training

An evaluation of nine critical appraisal skills training workshops provided to SSDs within the CEBSS initiative suggests that this approach can give substantial short-term gains in self-reported understanding, although long-term gains were not assessed. The workshops were based on the Critical Appraisal Skills Programme (CASP) methods, which originated in health care and were adapted for use within SSDs through initial pilot work. Participants rated the workshops well and more than two thirds reported an interest in getting involved in further critical appraisal skills training (**B7**).

More generally, front–line staff report a lack of departmental support or encouragement for keeping abreast of research (for example, **A1**). The extent to which research is discussed in supervision appears to vary widely, and there is some uncertainty about the value of this approach (**A1**, **A3**; **B1**, **B3**; **S/I**). Some studies report pockets of a 'culture of antipathy' to research within social care that runs counter to the culture required to underpin the research–based practitioner model (**A4**; **B3**, **B5**). Negative attitudes towards research also sometimes emerged in seminars, particularly among practitioners and with reference to the independent care sector. The lack of a professional career structure in the independent care sector was seen as an impediment to individuals accessing and using research by some fieldwork respondents.

Although its focus is on using research in group discussions, the study detailed in the box below provides some insight into the workings, and potential failings, of the research–based practitioner model (**A6**).

Improving services for the over-50s

This research brought together two local multistakeholder groups and charged them with formulating policies to improve local services for the over-50s. Individual members were expected to locate and bring relevant information to the group, including research findings. The groups' librarians also passed on the results of literature searches requested by the groups.

The study found that research use by both groups failed to match the linear process assumed by the research-based practitioner model. Instead, certain forms of knowledge became accepted currency, primarily knowledge based on professional and personal experience rather than research knowledge. Some existing relevant research was never accessed by the groups and on occasions robust research findings presented at meetings were devalued. Although members possessed both critical appraisal skills and tools with which to assess the quality of new information brought to the groups, these were rarely used. Research was re-presented and 'transformed' through individuals' experiences or agendas or through synthesis with other forms of knowledge such as experience. Overall, research use was haphazard and opportunistic, and depended on both the organisational features of the groups, and on changing agendas, roles and power relations within them (**A6**).

3.2. The embedded research model

In the embedded research model, practitioners rarely engage directly with findings from research. Research enters practice by becoming embedded in the systems and processes of social care, through mechanisms such as standards of care, inspection frameworks, national and local policies and procedures, and practice tools. Research knowledge enters practitioner knowledge via policy community knowledge, or through its translation into practice activities. However, other forms of knowledge may influence the guidance and practice tools that are produced, particularly the tacit and experiential knowledge of both practitioners and service users.

In this model, the key link is thus not between research and practice, but between research and policy. The responsibility for developing and ensuring research-informed practice lies with local and national policy makers and service delivery managers, who translate key messages from research into governance frameworks, guidance and practice tools. The underlying view of research use is again a linear one, where existing research is accessed and used instrumentally in the design of social care processes and practices.

The embedded research model does not require high levels of practice autonomy, and in fact may restrict this. To be effective, the model's approach depends on widespread adoption of research-informed guidance and tools. Adoption may be encouraged or demanded by, for example, performance measurement, inspection and appraisal regimes.

The eLSC's BPGs (described in Chapter 2) provide an example of a national-level activity that reflects the embedded research model approach. The guides combine research knowledge with that of service users, carers and practitioners. Research-based practice tools and protocols have also been developed in local contexts, for example the *Ten pitfalls* practice booklet and accompanying referral chart developed from Department of Health research on child protection[30]. However, this model remains relatively undeveloped as yet within the UK.

In terms of its likely effectiveness, there is some evidence that senior officials have better access to research than practitioners, and of support for the view that policy documents should explicitly reference findings from research (**A3**, **A4**). Our seminars found that research was more likely to be valued at policy level, and respondents felt research was better targeted at those with strategic, planning and policy development responsibilities than at front-line practitioners. However, there were also concerns among seminar participants about research-informed practice becoming centrally dictated.

Where research is embedded in policies and guidance, the barriers that practitioners face in accessing and understanding research (see the research-based practitioner model) are no longer relevant, although some individual policy makers may still face these barriers. The embedded research approach may also minimise problems created by negative attitudes to research, as practitioners need not be aware that policies and guidance are informed by research.

However, cross-sector reviews of initiatives to promote research use provide some warning messages about the likely success of an embedded research model within social care (**A7**, **A8**; **B8**). They offer strong evidence, primarily from the health care field, that guidance alone does not change practice and needs to be supported by additional activities, for example education or training. Guidelines are an increasing feature of human services within North America. However, there is some small-scale evidence that awareness and especially use of practice guidelines by human services staff in Canada and the US is low, and that social workers may be more inclined to use guidelines based on professional consensus than those supported by research (**A9**, **A10**).

Cross-sector reviews (**A7**, **A8**; **B8**) conclude that one of the keys to developing research-informed practice is ensuring ownership of the research by potential users. This sense of ownership may sometimes be limited within the embedded research model where practitioners do not engage directly with the research or its development into guidance and tools. However, studies of initiatives to develop research-based practice tools suggest that practitioner engagement with the research can occur at the development stage (see below).

Care management with older people

The implementation of a new research-based form for recording intended outcomes in care management with older people was trialled. The form was developed collaboratively between researchers and social care staff using an approach that aimed to establish ownership of these new ways of working.

The trial implementation involved 12 staff, including social workers, care managers, senior practitioners and home care organisers, recruited and briefed by care managers who were involved in the planning group. Staff reported positive effects of the forms on their practice although completed forms showed some variation in the extent to which they were used successfully. The forms are now being adopted across the whole local authority (**A11**).

To be successful, research-based tools may need to fit the local practice context, in terms of: available resources, the extent to which they tackle locally recognised problems, and their integration with other activities (**A11**). New tools also need to fit with the client group concerned (**B2**). 'Time out' to explore the issues around using the tools and to practise new methods of working appears to support their successful introduction (**A12**; **B2**). Conversely, lack of time inhibits staff capacity to take on and learn about new tools and tasks (**A11**, **A12**; **B2**). However, research-based practice tools do seem to support changes in both knowledge and practice (**A11**, **A12**; **B2**, see below).

Research-based checklists for looked-after children

Research-based practice checklists were introduced to nine local authority SSDs. The checklists were initially developed through a consultation process with potential checklist users, but most authorities took them 'blind', without being involved in their development. Implementation was supported by varying levels of training.

Overall, checklists were completed for half of relevant cases, but there was much variation. Use of checklists also declined over time. In general, more intensive models of intervention gave higher completion rates, but there were exceptions. The majority of those who completed the booklets found them useful, and felt they had increased knowledge of the issues around looked-after children (**B2**).

3.3. The organisational excellence model

In the organisational excellence model, the key to developing research–informed practice lies not with individual practitioners or policy makers, but with social care organisations: their leadership, management and organisation. This approach recognises that the actions of individual practitioners, even those who are professionally qualified, are shaped and constrained by the local management and structure of social care, and by the culture of the organisation.

Social care organisations are undertaking a wide range of activities to facilitate research use: specific HRM activities, such as changes in job descriptions and new 'boundary spanning' research-practice posts, appraisal and reward systems, research-based training, and team management practices, such as setting time aside to discuss research in meetings. Above all, initiatives to promote research use within this model focus on changing the culture of the organisation, as embodied in the ways social care organisations are led and managed.

The organisational excellence model focuses on adapting and learning from research at the organisational level to reflect local circumstances and priorities. The organisation is not seen as merely a conduit for getting externally generated research findings to impact on practice. Organisational learning is to the fore, through local experimentation, evaluation and practice development based on research. Research knowledge thus becomes integrated with organisational knowledge. To facilitate this, partnerships are being forged with local universities and with other intermediary organisations, such as RiP and MRC.

The view of research use underpinning the organisational excellence model is thus cyclical rather than linear. The focus is on local adaptation of research findings and the approach is often collaborative, with joint production of knowledge between researchers and practitioners. Practitioner knowledge becomes integrated with research knowledge in a much more dynamic and interactive process, through testing out research findings and shaping them to local contexts and experience. 'Use' of research is part of, not separate from, this process of knowledge creation.

The role of service users in the organisational excellence model is, however, less clear from the activities and initiatives we uncovered for this review. Despite this there is potential for service users to become involved as active partners alongside researchers and practitioners in shaping research knowledge to local contexts of care, in implementing interventions informed by research, or as participants in action research projects.

We might expect that activities undertaken by SSDs to promote research use would broadly fit with this organisational excellence model. The documents provided directly by SSDs do suggest a good deal of activity along these lines. Partnerships are being developed with local universities through conducting research, secondments and joint appointments, the provision of research-based training and expert advice, and the overall development of a culture that is open to the use of research. A range of different intermediary posts have been created and practice and staff development activities are also reported. There is an indication from documents from some SSDs that the use of research is becoming integrated with existing organisational processes, priorities and ways of thinking, for example as a theme within wider strategy documents.

In some areas these developments are combined with approaches that better reflect the research–based practitioner model. This mainly involves improving access to research for individual practitioners, through better library provision, Internet access, guides to searching the literature and local research databases, and sometimes critical appraisal skills training as well. Where overall strategies for promoting the use of research have been developed by SSDs, these sometimes include elements of both the organisational excellence and research–based practitioner models.

The evidence uncovered by the review suggests there may be strong support for developing research-informed practice in line with the organisational excellence model. It fits well with the widely reported view among social care staff that ensuring research feeds into service delivery processes is a joint responsibility between organisations and individuals (**A1, A2, A3; B10; S/I**). Social care staff also generally believe that the research-informed practice agenda should be led from the top within departments and agencies (**A2**, **A3**; **B5**). Seminar respondents emphasised the key role of senior managers in developing research use, in enthusing individuals and in modelling research-based change.

Cross-sector reviews (**A7**, **A8**) conclude that strong and visible leadership is crucial to initiatives to promote the use of research. However, social care staff seem uncertain as to who are or should be crucial leaders in taking forward research-informed practice within agencies. Suggestions have included operational and senior managers, policy/planning staff, research staff, training staff and practice development posts (**A2**). The importance of local research 'champions' was recognised in the seminars and is supported by good evidence from cross-sector reviews (**A7**, **A8**).

In a small-scale study, management, research and policy staff identified a number of barriers to leading research-informed practice within social care (**A2**):

- lack of time, resources and sometimes skills;
- instability within departments;
- isolation within departments in terms of driving a research use agenda forward;
- potential role conflicts between 'policing' compliance with operational processes and encouraging staff to question practice;
- lack of evidence that research use makes a difference to service users.

The review uncovered very little evidence about the role of teams in developing research-informed practice in social care. Senior personnel within SSDs appear to support the view that teams are important in driving change, but question the extent to which they should take responsibility for this particular agenda (**A3**). Team managers report that they view research as important to practice although they do not tend to access research on a regular basis; and there is some support for discussing research in team meetings (**B3**, **B11**). Seminar respondents felt lack of time inhibits discussion of research within team meetings.

In terms of staff development, findings were mixed. Social care staff acknowledge the value of research-based training in developing research-informed practice, but the extent to which training is currently based on research is unclear (**B1**, **B3**, **B4**, **B11**). Seminar respondents noted that the absence of a career structure in the independent care sector, coupled with lack of motivation for personal development, restricts the value of staff development approaches for developing research-informed practice within this staff group.

Evidence to support the value of research-practice partnerships to develop research-informed social care is limited. However, cross-sector reviews conclude that collaborative approaches have proved successful in other sectors. They also emphasise the importance of personal contacts between researchers and users if research is to be used (**A7, A8**). Seminar respondents felt dialogue between researchers and practitioners was important for securing research-informed practice, and the literature also reports that social care staff view such partnerships positively (**B5, B6**). However, some believe that a 'blame culture' may inhibit the experimentation and innovation that underpins this model (**A3**).

Our seminars reported positive support for research involving practitioners, which was viewed as more relevant to practice and valued more highly. Cross-sector reviews have found that internally conducted and commissioned research is more likely to be seen as relevant by potential users (**A7, A8**). The cost of commissioning research locally may, however, present a barrier (**B5**).

Cross-sector reviews conclude that initiatives to promote research use need to be integrated with existing organisational processes and priorities (**A7, A8**), and seminar respondents felt this was important within social care. The following example, derived from an evaluation of a initiative to promote research-based practice, outlines some other features that may contribute to the success of an organisational excellence approach.

Key worker services

A project to develop multiagency research-based key worker services for families with disabled children within two local authority SSDs provides an example of working within the organisational excellence model to promote research use. A research team worked closely with each site's multiagency steering group. Three 'reflective' workshops disseminated research information on key working and supported the development of action plans and their implementation. Between workshops, the research team provided ongoing support for managers and fed into training for key workers.

Some of the features that contributed to successful implementation were:

- the role of the research team in supporting the processes of planning and implementation, both practically and by maintaining momentum for the project;
- opportunities to share learning across sites at managerial level;
- a small-scale, learning approach to implementation, allowing time for reflection;
- 'time out' for managers provided by workshops;
- managerial commitment, providing high level support and status and acting as champions for the project;
- sustaining motivation, among both management and front-line staff;
- supportive features within local contexts of implementation;
- adequate training and supervision, and dedicated time for these;
- good communication between managers and front-line staff;
- a project coordinator who acted as line manager to front-line staff, provided a link with high level management and coordinated overall effort (**A13**).

Action research projects also provide examples of working within an organisational excellence model: research is undertaken in local contexts, based on local problems, and targets for action are set as part of an interactive process between research and practice. Overall, the action research projects identified by the review appeared to be successful to some degree in changing practice (**A14**; **B12**), but not all projects met their aims (**B13**).

The three models outlined above have been identified from current strategies and initiatives to promote research-informed practice in social care. Despite this, our literature searches and fieldwork found that evidence of the effectiveness of these models is largely absent. There is also very limited evidence about potential barriers and enablers to their development.

The models are useful because they help clarify the ways in which research-informed practice is being developed in the social care sector, and the assumptions and implications that underlie different approaches. At the same time, the picture on the ground is inevitably less straightforward. The models are not mutually exclusive and practices often combine the ideas of more than one model. Questions of gaps, tensions and possible synergies between the models are addressed in Chapter 4. In the remainder of this chapter, we briefly examine conceptual frameworks for research use in social care identified in the theoretical literature. This enables us to explore whether our empirically based models reflect these wider discussions.

3.4. Conceptual frameworks of research use

While the three models outlined above are based on current activities in the UK social care sector, it would be naive to assume that such initiatives take place in a vacuum. Their development is likely to be influenced by key debates and thinking in the field, whether directly or indirectly. Such debates are captured in the conceptual literature identified by the review.

An examination of this conceptual literature uncovered five broad frameworks for thinking about and developing research-informed practice in social care. These are briefly described below, in order to examine the extent to which our three empirical models reflect explicit conceptual ideas about using research in social care practice.

The evidence-based practitioner framework: this framework derives from the evidence-based medicine (EBM) approach developed within health care[194]. Research-informed social care is defined as "the conscientious, explicit and judicious use of current best evidence in making decisions regarding the welfare of those in need"[154]. It involves the integration of research knowledge with practitioner knowledge and with the experiences and preferences of service users to make decisions. Research use is seen as a rational, linear process in which individual practitioners access, appraise and apply research findings to a practice problem. The commitment to explicitness means practitioners work in an open and contractual way with service users who are actively involved in the decision making process (see, for example, [6,95,136,154,156]).

This framework broadly mirrors our research-based practitioner model.

The multiple influence framework: this is a more pragmatic way of thinking which questions the ideal of the rational use of research and instead recognises that multiple influences shape social care practice:

- the moral, legal and political context;
- pragmatics – what is possible as well as what ought to be done;
- the views of service users; and
- research.

Here, research-informed social care means creating a balance between these different influences. It provides a conceptual framework that reconciles all the influences on practice, and into which new ideas, research findings and projects can be fitted. Different influences on practice may not be complementary and the interaction between them is often complex. Further, moral, legal, political, pragmatic and service user issues are likely to become enmeshed in research. The multiple influence framework recognises the values that underpin the use of research and research knowledge itself. Where the evidence-based practitioner framework tends to foreground research knowledge in making decisions, the multiple influence framework recognises that any influence may come to the fore in decision making in any particular context. This includes the views of service users (see, for example, [23,87,180,181]).

The multiple influence framework represents a conceptual stance towards using research in social care as much as providing a substantive outline of how research-informed practice might be developed. As such it does not readily map onto any one of our empirical models. However, its more pragmatic approach and its doubt about the possibility of straightforwardly rational use of research means this framework has some parallels with the organisational excellence model.

The supported implementation framework: this framework places an emphasis on the implementation of research that goes beyond a focus on individual practitioners accessing and consuming research. Implementation means supporting practitioners to apply research or research-based technologies, including guidelines. This might involve technical assistance, training or supportive IT systems. A key concern rests on the degree to which research use involves the precise replication of interventions found to be effective, or local adaptation to circumstances. While the literature does not generally identify a role for service users in this framework, they might contribute to the development of guidelines and other research-based technologies and tools (see, for example, [37,68,69,83,147,177,178,180,190]).

This framework links most closely with our embedded research model, in which research is implemented through social care systems, guidance and practice tools.

The linkage and exchange framework: this framework views the use of research as a complex, non-linear process, where there is interaction and flow of information between researchers and practitioners. Practitioners are not simply passive recipients of research, but actively negotiate and reconstruct research findings through their own knowledge and experience. The focus is on collaboration between practitioners and researchers to address practice questions and produce 'practice-based evidence'. Action learning methods are advocated that promote democratic participation in the shaping and use of knowledge. Again, while service users are not typically mentioned in this framework, they might be involved in conducting and/or participating in the development of 'practice-based evidence', for example as stakeholders within communities of practice (see, for example, [12,46,58,59,64,99,179,180,181]).

This framework has clear parallels with the approach of the organisational excellence model, in its focus on partnerships and the collaborative production of research knowledge.

The scientifically based practice framework: this framework proposes the use of research *methods* to shape practice activities. As such, its focus is somewhat different from that of this review, which examines the use of empirical findings from research. Here, practitioners apply scientific ideas and methods to individual cases, and use research techniques to assess and evaluate their own practice. At its most extreme, this approach rests on:

- the use of 'single subject design' methodologies in which baseline data on a client's problem are compared with data following intervention; and
- the use of standardised rapid assessment instruments to monitor symptoms and evaluate outcomes.

This very specific approach has been subject to critique and does not appear to have been widely used even within the US where it originated.

It has also been suggested that it downplays the relationship between the practitioner and the service user, and the role of service users within this model is unclear[81,83,138,175]. However, the framework does begin to point towards a wider literature on the use of research methods to develop practice, that includes issues such as evaluating practice and reflective learning. It highlights the value of a different aspect of research–practice integration: that of researching practice itself.

This framework has no clear parallels with the models we identified which focus on the use of findings from research, and not the use of research methods.

Debates in the conceptual literature are often focused on defining the nature and status of knowledge from research, and on the relationship between this research knowledge and practitioner knowledge (for example,[47,83,180,181]). In terms of research knowledge, a key question arises about whether knowledge from certain types of study should be seen as superior to others (for example, [71,86,98,181]). Similarly, a core theme to emerge from our analysis across the empirical studies and seminars was the expressed need for a consensus as to what counts as 'evidence', or knowledge, within the social care field. These are complex issues, which have been the subject of other work commissioned by SCIE[1].

4

A whole systems approach to research use

Our review has documented the way in which the various initiatives and activities designed to promote research use are underpinned by three broad ways of thinking about research use: the research-based practitioner, the embedded research and the organisational excellence models. Although these models were presented separately in Chapter 3, they are not mutually exclusive. Any single initiative might draw on more than one model at different stages within its development.

Carer assessment and review

The project used findings from initial research with service users, carers, practitioners and managers within two local authority SSDs to implement an outcomes approach to carer assessment and review. Planning for the project and briefing and training events were undertaken collaboratively and included service users. Fourteen staff in one local authority piloted the assessment forms.

On evaluation, practitioners said that they found the assessment forms useful in supporting practice and in helping raise awareness and understanding of relevant issues. They also reported improvements in practice, which were supported by written records. Carers made a number of positive comments about the new assessment process but also identified some room for improvement.

Although the project broadly represents an example of an 'organisational excellence' approach to developing research-informed practice, the assessment forms it developed reflect a more 'embedded research' approach, in which individual practitioners using the tools need not engage with their underpinning research base (**A12**).

The models are grounded in a range of emergent initiatives to promote the use of research in social care. Yet such initiatives do not appear to have developed in a coordinated way. Evidence on the efficacy of each of the models is also limited. Thus, it is not clear whether the models can comfortably coexist, or whether there are potential tensions and contradictions between them.

To analyse these issues, we have adopted a whole systems approach to thinking about research use in the social care sector. It proposes that research use involves more than single individuals or single organisations acting in isolation. To understand research use in social care, we need instead to examine the interconnections between different people and organisations, and any synergy, or potential conflicts, that might arise between them. A systems approach assumes that initiatives to improve the use of research are more likely to be successful if they complement one another and if, together, they address the whole social care system.

Our models suggest that a systems approach to thinking about research use is relevant. Both individually and together they highlight the variety of people and organisations involved in developing research-informed practice, the different roles they can play, and the importance of developing well-functioning relationships between them. A whole systems approach to analysis means considering further the relationships between the three models in order to develop a holistic and inclusive view of research use in social care: one that places the models within their wider context. It allows us to examine the broader implications of models, and the extent to which they engage all the relevant stakeholders in the research use process.

Our first step in adopting a whole systems approach involves identifying the main components of the social care system (people and organisations) that potentially have a role to play in research use. We then explore how the three models 'fit' within the social care system, particularly looking at the main roles identified in each model for people and organisations within the sector. We also examine whether the models are likely to sit comfortably together, any potential conflicts or tensions between them, and any gaps in the system that the models do not cover. The analysis is based on empirical evidence about the models where this exists, and on the assumptions that underpin the models.

4.1. The social care system

Figure 1 outlines six main categories of organisations and people within the social care system who potentially have a role to play in developing research use:

- governance and related organisations;
- research funders, research organisations and researchers;
- practice organisations, practice managers and practitioners;
- training organisations and trainers (including Sector Skills Councils in the future);
- service user representative organisations and service users;
- facilitating organisations and individual facilitators.

There is a range of governance and related organisations involved directly or indirectly in the promotion of research use. Our focus here is on the general features of the infrastructure for social care for England, Wales and Northern Ireland – the areas under SCIE's remit. As part of the programme to modernise social services, this new infrastructure for quality includes:

- Care Standards organisations, responsible for ensuring that care services meet national minimum standards determined by central government (note that, in England, from 1 April 2004, the National Care Standards Commission [NCSC] and the Social Services Inspectorate [SSI] are now combined in a new Commission for Social Care Inspection [CSCI]);
- the Care Councils, responsible for regulating the social care workforce and for promoting high standards of practice and training within the social care workforce;
- organisations for social care employers to take responsibility for training needs analysis, a national training strategy, workforce planning, national occupational standards, and the national qualifications framework for social care (such as, in England, Topss – soon to become a Sector Skills Council);
- SCIE, which is responsible for developing and promoting knowledge about what works in social care.

Figure 1: The social care system and research use

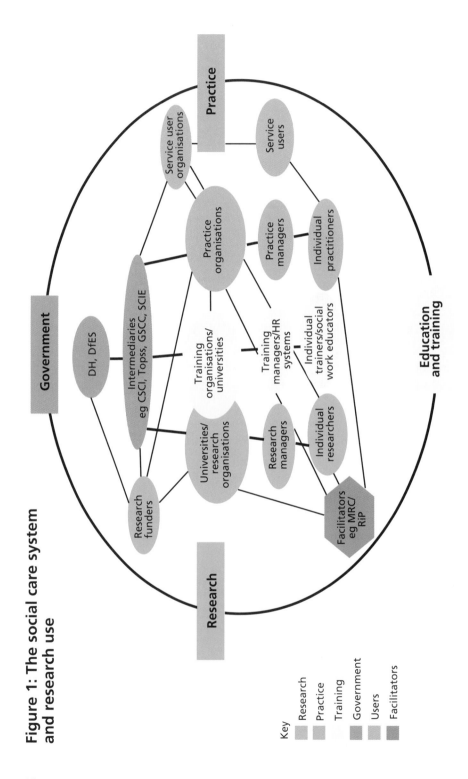

These national governance organisations not only relate to one another but also interact with and impact on research funders (government research and development programmes, research councils and charitable trusts); research providers (primarily university researchers); training organisations (including universities) and trainers; and practice organisations and practitioners.

Social care is characterised by the diverse range of organisations involved in the delivery of care, including not only SSDs but also private and voluntary sector care homes and care services. The social care workforce is likewise fragmented and ranges from professionally qualified social workers to non-professionally qualified care home assistants. It is estimated that about 90% of the social care workforce is not professionally qualified[195].

An important aspect of the social care system, in relation to understanding research use, is the growth of a range of facilitating organisations (such as RiP, MRC, CEBSS and the ICCR), whose primary role is to promote and enable research-informed practice. They form a bridge between universities and researchers on the one hand, and practice organisations and practitioners on the other.

Last, but not least, there are service user organisations, service users, and their supporters and carers. They may contribute to research knowledge generation and also act as potential consumers of this knowledge. The governance framework for social care requires that organisations such as SCIE take account of the experience of those who use social care services and build this into their reviews of what works. Service user representative organisations are important communicators of these experiences. They also provide one means by which service users can become informed about research findings relating to what works in their areas of concern.

The social care system does not operate in isolation. Increasingly, policy staff, service delivery managers and front-line practitioners are required to contribute to the provision of joined-up services and work in an integrated way with others within the broader social policy system. In some instances this means that those involved in the delivery of social care are not managed on a day-to-day basis by social care staff.

A whole systems approach to research use envisages that the system will perform best (that is, deliver research-informed practice) if all parts of the system work together in complementary ways. It is, therefore, useful to consider which parts of the social care system the three models of research use focus on and what interactions each model advocates.

4.2. Mapping the three models of research use on to the social care system

Figures 2, 3 and 4 illustrate which parts of the social care system are assumed to be central to the research-based practitioner, embedded research and organisational excellence models of research use.

In the research-based practitioner model the focus is on the use of research by individual practitioners. This involves developing a positive attitude towards the value of research among practitioners and improving their search and critical appraisal skills. It also involves making research accessible to practitioners. Thus the people and organisations assumed to be central to this model are individual practitioners, training organisations (educators and trainers), and facilitating organisations (such as CEBSS) (see Figure 2). The ways in which these core people and organisations interact are seen as crucial to the success of the model. However, these core interactions may be enabled (or indeed hindered) by the actions of practice managers and intermediary organisations (such as the Care Councils and SCIE) who play supporting roles within this model. Researchers also play a potentially supporting role by ensuring that they write up their research findings in ways that are accessible to practitioners.

In the embedded research model the focus is on developing research-based guidance and practice tools, at either national or local levels, and establishing a governance framework that encourages or ensures the implementation of this guidance. At the national level, central government departments and intermediary organisations (such as CSCI) are assumed to play a central role (Figure 3). At the local level, it is practice organisations that have a key role in developing and adopting guidance, and in ensuring its implementation. Supporting roles are played by practice managers and facilitating organisations (such as MRC), who may be involved both in the development of research-based practice tools and in facilitating their implementation.

In the organisational excellence model, practice organisations and practice managers play a central role and hence they are emphasised in Figure 4. In many expressions of this model, practice organisations work

Figure 2: The research-based practitioner model and the social care system

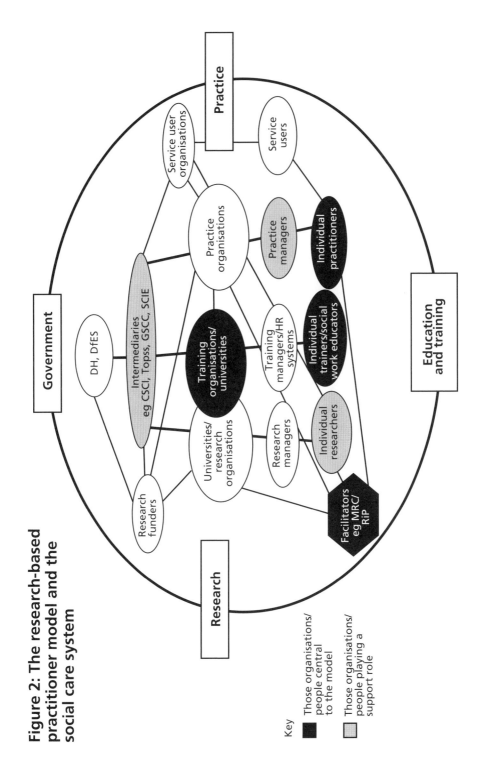

Key

■ Those organisations/ people central to the model

▨ Those organisations/ people playing a support role

Figure 3: The embedded research model and the social care system

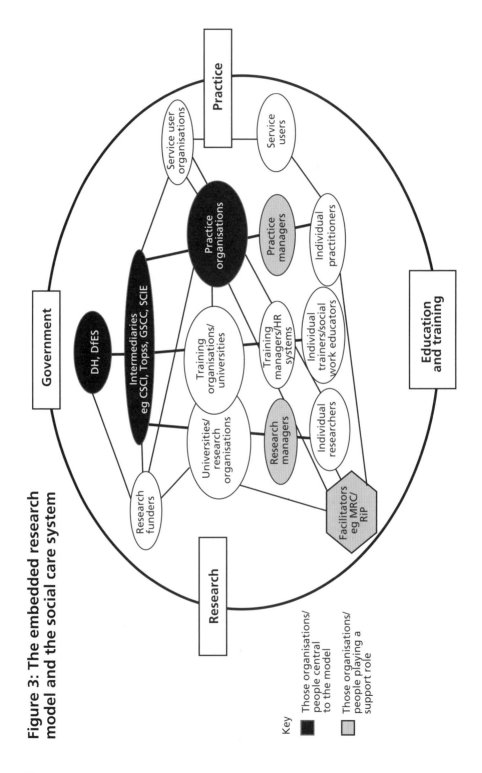

Key

Those organisations/ people central to the model

Those organisations/ people playing a support role

Figure 4: The organisational excellence model and the social care system

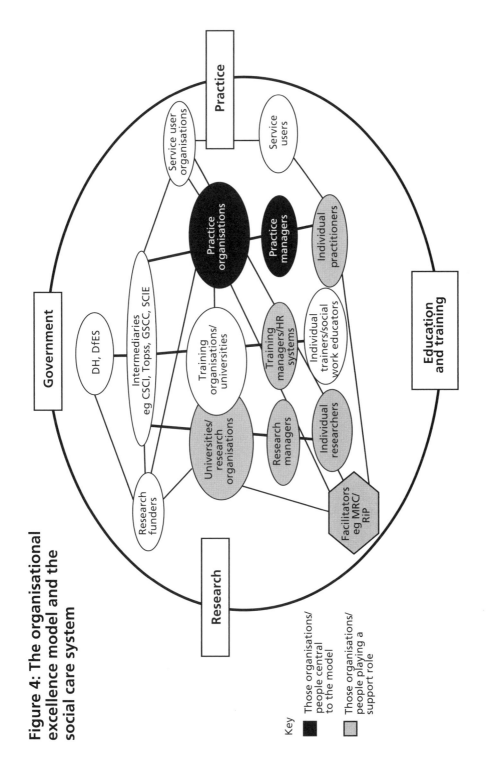

Key

■ Those organisations/ people central to the model

▨ Those organisations/ people playing a support role

in partnership with facilitating organisations (such as RiP) or with research organisations and individual researchers. Although the latter are shown in Figure 4 as playing a supporting role, it is arguable that their role is more central. Training and HRM systems also play a supporting role in this model, particularly in relation to developing a 'research-minded' culture.

Looking across the maps of all three models, it is possible to consider the extent to which they complement each other, and hence whether the system is likely to perform at its best where these models coexist. To address this issue four main questions are considered in the remainder of this chapter:

1. Are there tensions between the models and, more particularly, where organisations and people play a central role in more than one model, are these roles compatible?
2. Do the three models ignore parts of the social care system and, if so, do these omissions need to be addressed?
3. Are different models suited to different circumstances?
4. What are the implications of the above for developing a whole systems approach to promoting research use?

Our analysis below takes account of both evidence on the effectiveness and appropriateness of the models (outlined in Chapter 3), and the assumptions that underpin the models.

4.3. Tensions

Practice managers and facilitating organisations play key roles in all three models of research use. The key issue is whether there are tensions between the roles they are expected to perform under each model.

It appears as if practice managers may experience role conflict if faced with a combination of all three models, although none of the empirical studies uncovered by this review addressed this issue. In the research-based practitioner model they facilitate research use by individual practitioners. They do this by encouraging staff to take personal responsibility for research use, by enabling practitioners to develop critical appraisal skills, by providing access to library and IT systems, and by ensuring that supervision sessions draw on research to inform decisions.

However, the role of practice managers is different under the embedded research model. Now the manager rather than the practitioner has more responsibility for ensuring that service delivery is informed by research. The key messages from research need to be incorporated into practice guidance and tools. The managerial task is then either to encourage practitioner use of these tools, or to ensure that practitioners do in fact use them (a more coercive approach).

Both the research-based practitioner and the embedded research models incorporate a linear view of research use, where emphasis is placed on the adoption of research findings rather than their creation and adaptation. In contrast, in the organisational excellence model the practice manager's task is more wide-ranging, including the local adaptation of existing research, the commissioning of research locally, and the establishment of ongoing development and evaluation activities. All of these activities are often undertaken in partnership with others. In addition, the manager's relationship with practitioners involves team working rather than the one-to-one relationship implied in the research-based practitioner model, or the somewhat impersonal interaction implied in the embedded research model.

The role for facilitating organisations likewise varies in each of the models. In the research-based practitioner model, they act as trainers and coaches for practitioners, enabling them to access and understand research. In the embedded research model, their role is to develop research-based guidance and/or assist local practice organisations in developing their own guidance and practice tools. Finally, in the organisational excellence model facilitating organisations have a potentially wide-ranging set of roles, including acting as coach, trainer, consultant and research partner. There are likely to be tensions between these roles but these may be eased by the ways in which different facilitating organisations specialise in sub-sets of these activities.

In general, then, there are likely to be tensions between:

- the assumption of professional autonomy which underpins the research-based practice model, and the constraints placed on individual practitioners which may result from the embedded research model;
- an approach that emphasises a rather linear view of research use (the research-based practitioner and embedded research models) and a collaborative approach to the creation and use of research knowledge (the organisational excellence model).

These tensions may be felt most acutely at the practice level. However, they are also likely to permeate into the dilemmas faced by governance organisations when designing regulatory systems, and into how training organisations develop training strategies and learning opportunities.

4.4. Omissions

There are two parts of the social care system that do not feature strongly in any of our three models: research funders, and service users and their representative organisations.

Engaging research funders as part of a system for enabling better research use would seem to be important. The perceived lack of appropriate research to support policy and practice in social care was a recurring theme in studies in the literature and in the seminars and interviews. This is an issue that might be addressed by developing a national research and development strategy for social care. The absence of such a strategy contrasts markedly with parallel initiatives to enable research-informed practice in other sectors (such as health and education), where the identification of research priorities and the concentration of research resources on these priorities are considered to be crucial. However, the increasing focus on multidisciplinary working suggests that any research and development strategy for social care needs to ensure a joined-up approach to research on cross-cutting issues.

It would be unfair to argue that service users are entirely absent from the models. In the research-based practitioner model practitioners are encouraged to involve clients in a review of options, informed by research. Similarly, in the embedded research model guidance and tools may be based not only on findings from research but also on the experiences of those who use social care services. However, in neither of these models do service users or their representative organisations play a central role. By contrast, there are examples from health care of ways in which research-informed service users can play an important role in encouraging practice change by campaigning for certain research-based practices or by bringing particular research findings to the attention of individual practitioners[196,197].

4.5. Matching models to circumstances

We have already alluded to the possibility that different models may be best suited to different circumstances. Three possibilities are considered briefly here:

- that a different approach is required for professionally qualified social workers as opposed to the non-professionally qualified social care workforce;
- that different models might be relevant at different stages of a research development and implementation cycle;
- that different models might be relevant for different research questions/ findings.

In relation to the first of these issues, it might be assumed that the research-based practitioner model is best suited to the professionally qualified workforce and the embedded research model to the non-professionally qualified workforce. However, the evidence unearthed by this review would not seem to support this verdict. The research-based practitioner model does appear to be inappropriate for social care staff without professional qualifications, but it also seems to be rejected by many professionally qualified staff as well. Insofar as it provides a relevant model for the social care field, it needs to be applied more selectively. An adapted version of the research-based practitioner model may indeed be a more relevant model for policy makers (at national and local levels) rather than practitioners.

This should not, however, be interpreted as implying that the embedded research model is a panacea. Although it may provide a useful framework for promoting research use, particularly in the independent sector, the ways in which research-based guidance and practice tools are developed, adapted, implemented and updated needs further consideration.

This brings us neatly to the second issue of whether certain models are better suited to different stages of a research development and implementation cycle. The example that was cited at the beginning of this chapter suggests that this might be the case, but there is insufficient evidence to support the idea that models should be separated and labelled as either development or implementation models. The relationship between, for example, the embedded research model and organisational excellence model is likely to be more iterative than that.

Finally there is the issue of whether different models of research use are relevant for different research questions/findings. On the face of it, this would appear to make sense. Some research questions and projects, such as those that address the effectiveness of various social care practices, translate more readily into practice lessons. In all of our models there are ways that such research can be used. Other research questions and findings, such as those that focus on understanding social care problems from a service user perspective, may not lend themselves to being used in such an instrumental way. In this case research use relates more generally to reshaping the understandings of policy makers, service delivery organisations and front-line practitioners. This can be accommodated within the research-based practitioner and organisational excellence models, but it is difficult to see how the embedded research model would address the use of such research.

4.6. Developing a whole systems approach

The rationale for developing a whole systems approach is the assumption that initiatives to improve the use of research are more likely to be successful if they complement one another and if, together, they address the entire social care system.

Initiatives underpinned by any *one* of our three models will not achieve this and so there does seem to be a need to move forward on the basis of a combined approach. This will not be easy due to certain inherent tensions between the three models. In addition, these models have little to say about the roles that research funders and service users might play in improving research use, and action by both of these groups is potentially important.

To begin the process of developing a whole systems approach to research use, in Table 2 we outline the possible key roles and responsibilities of each of the six main categories of organisations and people within the social care system. This is, of necessity, speculative and it is an area where further work is required.

The development of a whole systems approach to research use is helpful in highlighting the potential complementarity of the three models identified by the review. However, it does assume the potential for developing a measure of consensus around research use. Although guidance for achieving consensus-based change is available in the literature on whole systems development[198], there are limitations to such an approach. Some of the controversies regarding research and its use in social care may signal a more fundamental dissent about the role of research, which is beyond the scope of the whole systems approach discussed in this chapter.

In this chapter we have addressed the issue of why it is helpful to think in terms of a whole systems approach to research use and what this entails. This highlights the need to consider the links between existing initiatives to improve the use of research and also begins to identify where further work is required. In Chapter 5 the implications of the review for research, policy and practice are considered in more detail.

Table 2: Developing a whole systems approach

Categories of organisations and people	Suggested key roles and responsibilities
Governance and related organisations	• Developing strategic frameworks – both for research and research use • Using research to inform policy, standards, protocols, inspection frameworks etc, and demonstrating the evidence base for each of these
Research funders	• Funding practice-relevant research • Encouraging user involvement in research planning (including service users) • Funding innovative dissemination, development and implementation strategies, and the evaluation of these
Research organisations and researchers	• Undertaking practice-relevant research • Providing overviews of extant research • Disseminating research in user-friendly formats

	• Working alongside practitioners and service users to identify local research needs
	• Developing collaborative links with practice organisations at local level
	• Supporting the conduct of research locally
Practice organisations, practice managers and practitioners	• Developing a culture of reflection, evaluation and learning in organisations
	• Providing resources/infrastructure to support research use
	• Ensuring local practice procedures and protocols are informed by research
	• Supporting continuing professional development in research use for key social care staff
	• Developing specific roles within organisation, such as practice development
	• Identifying practice-related research themes/problems, and referring them on to research funders and researchers
	• Ensuring HRM systems provide rewards and incentives for research use
	• Linking research use to other management processes such as the Performance Assessment Framework and Best Value
Training organisations and trainers	• Ensuring that training and continuing professional development are informed by up-to-date research
	• Using research regularly in training
	• Developing relevant training in research use and research conduct

Service user organisations and service users	• Identifying service user issues for research, and referring them on to research funders and researchers • Participating in research planning, design, execution and dissemination to ensure that research is informed by a service user perspective • Ensuring that campaigning activities are informed by research
Facilitating organisations	• Acting as a bridge between research and practice in diverse ways • Facilitating learning across practice organisations

5

Conclusions: implications and recommendations

Enhancing research use is an important aspect of developing a social care field – organisations and individuals – that wants to learn and evaluate the impact of what it does and make improvements. The experience of the health care sector would suggest that a research-informed practice agenda has the potential to:

- improve the quality, quantity and usefulness of research in social care;
- stimulate and support innovation and learning within social care;
- assist social care organisations in delivering on the Performance Assessment Framework.

This review has sought to understand how social care staff use research and how research use can be promoted and enhanced. It has done so by examining documented studies and current initiatives on research use, supplemented by fieldwork seminars and interviews to help address gaps in the literature. This chapter summarises the main conclusions, implications and recommendations to arise from this work.

Four key conclusions emerge from the review:

There is much activity within the social care field aimed at promoting and enhancing research use but this is often fragmented. Much of the activity occurs at the local level but there are also wider, regional and national, initiatives. The potential for an unknowing duplication of initiatives, with associated lost opportunities to learn from elsewhere, seems high. There would appear to be much that could be gained from better coordination of initiatives and activities.

The diversity of the social care field calls for a variety of actions to promote research use. Any coordination or streamlining of activity needs to recognise and respond to the diversity of the social care field, which encompasses a wide range of service delivery organisations, diverse client groups and a fragmented and largely non-professionally qualified workforce. Furthermore, many social care staff need to work in an integrated way with those in health and education services, and many work in multidisciplinary teams on multiagency projects and programmes.

Robust studies of what works in promoting research use in social care are few and far between. The potential to streamline and appropriately target activities to enhance research use depends on the availability of evidence about what works in this regard. However, evidence from published papers and practices detailed in documents received from SSDs suggests that although there is much activity on the ground, this has rarely been the subject of careful and robust evaluation. Of course, much of this activity is new, and evaluations may have yet to report. Where evaluations have been undertaken, these tend to focus on the professionally qualified workforce; there are large gaps in our understanding about how research and practice can be integrated for the non-professionally qualified workforce.

A whole systems approach to enhancing research use in social care appears to offer a positive way forward. Initiatives to promote research use within the social care field appear to be underpinned by three models of research use: the research-based practitioner, the embedded research and the organisational excellence models. Existing initiatives tend to be grounded in one of these models, although at different stages of development they may reflect either of the others. The models are important because they draw attention to different sets of assumptions about how research can and should be used to inform practice in social care. Although evidence about the likely effectiveness of each model is patchy, there are no grounds for uniquely preferring a research use strategy based on one model to the exclusion of the others. The ideas contained within each model are likely to be appropriate at different times and for different parts of the social care field. In enhancing research use, it is thus advantageous to think in terms of a whole systems approach, which blends and extends all three approaches and develops interconnected roles and responsibilities accordingly.

5.1. Implications for learning and HRM in social care

The review team was asked to draw out the implications of the review for approaches to learning and HRM by highlighting which approaches support the use of research in social care. In line with a whole systems approach, the review suggests that no single approach to learning or HRM will be appropriate for all social care staff. The following two boxes highlight the ways in which each of the three models of research use are supported by different forms of learning and HRM. It is important for the sector to ensure that no single learning or HRM approach is pursued to the exclusion of the others. However, the tensions inherent in employing multifaceted approaches also need to be managed carefully.

Implications for learning

In the *research-based practitioner model*, individually focused education and training on research use is emphasised. It is assumed that learning opportunities should focus on inculcating an approach that both values research and develops the knowledge and skills to access, understand and apply research in the conduct of day-to-day practice. This is reflected within the new degree in social work and the framework for post-qualifying training. Those who manage front-line practitioners also need to develop the knowledge and skills required to support the research-based practitioner model; the Advanced Award in Social Work provides one pathway by which these knowledge and skills might be gained.

In the *embedded research model*, some individuals need to develop the knowledge and skills required for accessing, understanding and applying research, especially those occupying policy and practice development roles. The development of 'application' knowledge and skills is particularly important: that is, how to translate research findings into practice procedures and tools. At present there appear to be few structured learning opportunities targeted at such needs: learning on the job appears to be the order of the day. There is scope for such training to be provided within the framework of requirements for post-qualifying awards, particularly the Advanced Award in Social Work. The model also implies that there will be a need for local training in the use of research-based tools, such as assessment forms and checklists.

In the *organisational excellence model*, the need for both individual and organisational learning is highlighted. The education and training needs of key individuals – those with practice development, research partnership and team management roles – are similar to those highlighted for the embedded research model. In addition, there is a need to develop the knowledge and skills that enable active involvement in research and evaluation projects. These latter needs are to some extent addressed in the framework of post-qualifying awards, particularly by the research pathway to the Advanced Award in Social Work. Over and above these individual learning requirements, there is also the need to develop an organisational learning approach (the subject of a separate SCIE project).

Implications for HRM

The research-based practitioner model is likely to be underpinned by an approach to HRM that provides the space and opportunity for individual learning and development. The requirement to ensure that individual practice is informed by research might be written into job descriptions, and could be a key criteria for determining career progression and other incentives and rewards.

The embedded research model is likely to be underpinned by a rather different HRM approach for the majority of social care staff. A key issue is how best to ensure that research-based practice procedures and tools are implemented appropriately by social care staff. The approach used may be based on developing a compliance framework, using management supervision, inspection and audit processes to encourage and ensure compliance. Alternatively, it may focus on encouraging and facilitating implementation, relying on training and incentives to achieve its ends.

The organisational excellence model is likely to be underpinned by an HRM approach that emphasises the important role that organisational leaders and line managers play in demonstrating and facilitating research use. The creation of specific posts and roles, such as practice development officers and research champions, may also be seen as crucial. Most importantly, flexible and supportive HRM practices are likely to be considered key to developing a learning organisation culture. In this regard, the facilitation of research use rather than compliance regimes are the order of the day.

Possibly the greatest danger of becoming too focused on a single model of research use arises in the area of learning. Much of the current emphasis relating to research use within the new social work degree and the associated framework for post-qualifying training is on developing the research-based practitioner. One of the key messages from the review is that not all members of the social care workforce need to be able to engage directly with research in order to ensure that it is used. Indeed, the development of specific skills in searching for and critically appraising research may be most appropriate for those with policy and practice development responsibilities. An ability to understand and engage with research findings may be an important means of encouraging a more general openness to research – a 'research minded' culture – but there is no evidence as yet on this.

Because of the recent focus of learning and training programmes on the research-based practitioner, much less attention seems to have been paid to the knowledge and skills required for implementing research-based recommendations – getting research into practice. This includes the knowledge and skills required for leading and managing research-informed practice initiatives within service delivery organisations. Recent reforms in the education and registration regimes of the social care workforce offer the potential to redress this balance. In particular, the overarching requirements for each of the four alternative pathways to the Advanced Award in Social Work appear to provide a framework for such developments.

One of the most difficult tensions to manage in developing a multifaceted, whole systems approach to research use, is that between *facilitating* research-informed practice on the one hand, and ensuring *compliance* with research-informed practices on the other. This presents significant challenges for HRM systems, particularly at the local level. More work is needed on whether and how research use is supported by incorporating it as a requirement within job descriptions, appraisal regimes, and career development and reward systems.

5.2. Future directions for research and development in research use and practice change in social care

Throughout this review, and specifically in Appendix 2, we have commented on the wide gaps in the existing evidence base on how research use can be promoted and enhanced within social care. The review found that studies of the use of research in social care have largely focused on:

• the professionally qualified workforce;
• managers and team leaders, and less often front-line staff;
• the use of research by individuals accessing, reading and applying research.

More research is needed around:

• how research and practice can be integrated for the non-professionally qualified workforce;
• other routes through which research impacts on practice in social care than through individuals directly accessing research, for example through policy and research-based training;
• the use of research at the organisational and system levels, not just among individuals;
• whether service user involvement in research or in the research utilisation process enhances the use of research.

Robust studies of what works in promoting research use in social care are few and far between. Of course, it is still early days in the drive for using research in social care practice, and outcomes cannot always yet be judged. Other research may be ongoing. This lack of evidence highlights the importance of learning from cross-sector research on promoting research use. Evidence from other sectors also suggests the value of alternative approaches and ideas for encouraging the use of research. Future work in social care needs to focus on:

- building some robust assessment of effectiveness into activities designed to promote the use of research;
- examining ways of promoting research use through the embedded research model. Key issues here are:
  - involving staff and service users in developing new protocols and tools;
  - the need for additional implementation strategies to ensure such protocols and tools are adopted.

Any future research and development work in this field will also need to attend to key issues raised by quality assessment of the studies selected as relevant for this review. The quality of these studies was often not judged to be high. In part this reflected poor reporting of methods or findings (see Appendix 2). However, a number of questions about the nature and quality of the evidence base in this field are also raised:

1. There is a lack of experimental studies to examine the effectiveness of interventions to promote research use. While findings from many different types of study can contribute to research-informed practice, some form of experimental approach is usually viewed as the most appropriate for measuring intervention effectiveness. However, the single study identified that did attempt an experimental approach (**B2**) found that it was difficult to use this method successfully within real world social care settings. Robust approaches to assessing the effectiveness of interventions to promote research utilisation need to be developed, that are both useful and suitable for the social care field. These should be supplemented by evaluations of the process through which such interventions can be successfully implemented.

2. The use of research is a complex phenomenon. Yet it is rare for studies to be lodged within a conceptual framework for understanding or assessing research utilisation. Few studies explicitly define what is meant by research use. They typically focus on individuals directly accessing and applying the findings from research, and most rely on subjective, self-report measures of use. However, research use can be a more subtle and complicated process, and practitioners may not be aware that their practice is informed by research. Future work needs to:

   - develop conceptual frameworks for understanding and assessing research use;

- establish clear definitions and measures of research use;
- develop objective as well as subjective measures of use.

3. A key aspect of using research in social care practice is that it involves the integration of research knowledge with other types of knowledge, such as practitioner knowledge. This may occur in different ways through the different routes by which research gets utilised. The nature of this integration is a key source of debate in the research utilisation field more widely[120]. However, only one of the 28 empirical studies whose findings were included in this review directly considers this issue (**A6**). It represents an important focus for further research.

4. Very few studies attempted to measure research use in terms of changes in ultimate outcomes for service users. Where this occurred, the influence of research on such outcomes proved difficult to assess (for example, **B2**). Future research and development work needs to examine the issues raised by measuring the impact of research on outcomes for service users, and whether alternative or proxy measures may also be appropriate.

The gaps in the research base and the issues raised about study quality highlight the lack of current robust evidence about how best to develop research-informed practice in the social care field. Future research and development work needs to be integrated with and build on the good quality studies that exist.

5.3. Recommendations

Three key recommendations for the social care field arise from the review:

- The social care field should, using this review as a starting point, take stock of current activities and initiatives to promote research use.
- An overarching framework for promoting and developing research use in social care is required and the whole systems approach, outlined in Chapter 4, is recommended.
- In order to ensure that initiatives to promote research use are themselves based on evidence, a research and development agenda on these issues needs to be articulated and pursued. This should build on the future directions for research and development outlined in this chapter.

SCIE has an important role to play in driving and facilitating action in all of these areas. Developing a whole systems approach is likely to be central to future initiatives but this should not be envisaged as a mechanical exercise. Living systems are not wholly predictable, nor do they exist in isolation. Although key people and organisations within the social care system can exert significant influence on the ways in which the system as a whole evolves, they cannot control this process.

References

For readers wishing to investigate in more depth some of the conceptual discussions about research utilisation, within social care and more widely, the following papers provide useful introductions:

- For examples of discussions and debate about developing research-informed social care within the UK, see papers first authored by Atherton[6,7], Bullock et al[23], Lewis[86-9], Macdonald[94], Macdonald and Sheldon[98], Sheldon[152-3], Sheldon and Chilvers[154-5], Sheldon and Macdonald[156] and Webb[180-1]; and within North America, see papers by Gambrill[47-9] and Kirk and Reid[83].
- The papers first authored by Bullock et al[23], Nutley and Davies[116,117], Nutley et al[118-20], Sanderson[148], Walter et al[176-7] and Weiss[184-7] discuss wider issues of using research in public sector policy and practice, including questions such as types of knowledge and types of research use, and different models of research utilisation.
- The National Center for the Dissemination of Disability Research (NCDDR) papers[110-13] provide a useful introduction to issues around research dissemination.
- The guidelines debate in social care within the US is considered in the papers first authored by Howard and Jeffrey[68] and Howard and Jenson[69], Kirk[81] and Richey and Roffman[142].
- Papers that have developed a clear conceptual framework for a methodology for measuring research use include those first authored by Bullock et al[23], Molas-Gallart et al[105] and Landry et al[84-5].

1. Pawson, R., Boaz, A., Grayson, L., Long, A. and Barnes, C. (2003) *Types and quality of knowledge in social care*, SCIE Knowledge Review 3, London: SCIE (November).
2. Albery, S. (2002) 'Developing a mental health promotion strategy in Croydon: the voluntary sector perspective', *Journal of Mental Health Promotion*, vol 1, no 3, pp 27-9.
3. Alsop, A. (1997) 'Evidence-based practice and continuing professional development', *British Journal of Occupational Therapy*, vol 60, no 11, pp 503-8.

4   Anderson, M., Cosby, J., Swan, B., Moore, H. and Broekhoven, M. (1999) 'The use of research in local health service agencies', *Social Science and Medicine*, vol 49, no 8, pp 1007-19.

5   Anderson, S.G. (2001) 'The collaborative research process in complex human services agencies: identifying and responding to organizational constraints', *Administration in Social Work*, vol 25, no 4, pp 1-19.

6   Atherton, C. (1999) 'Getting a GRIP', *Research Policy and Planning*, vol 17, no 1, pp 1-4.

7   Atherton, C. (2002) 'Changing culture not structure: five years of research in practice in child care', *MCC: Building Knowledge for Integrated Care*, vol 10, no 1, pp 17-21.

8   Atwal, A. (2002) 'Getting evidence into practice: the challenges and successes of action based research', *British Journal of Occupational Therapy*, vol 56, no 7, pp 335-41. (**B13**)

9   Banks, C.K. and Wildeman, G. (1996) '"The company of neighbours": building social support through the use of ethnography', *International Social Work*, vol 39, no 3, pp 317-28.

10   Bannigan, K. and Hooper, L. (2002) 'How journal clubs can overcome barriers to research utilization', *British Journal of Therapy and Rehabilitation*, vol 9, no 8, pp 299-303.

11   Barnes, V., Clouder, L., Hughes, C., Purkis, J. and Pritchard, J. (2000) *Dissemination as evidence? Deconstructing the processes of disseminating qualitative research*, Qualitative Evidence-based Practice Conference, Coventry University, 15-17 May.

12   Barratt, M. (2002) 'Real evidence-based practice development: a partnership approach', *MCC: Building Knowledge for Integrated Care*, vol 10, no 6, pp 9-14.

13   Barratt, M. (2003) 'Organizational support for evidence-based practice within child and family social work: a collaborative study', *Child and Family Social Work*, vol 8, no 2, pp 143-50. (**A3**)

14   Bartels, S.J., Haley, W.E. and Dums, A.R. (2002) 'Implementing evidence based practices in geriatric mental health', *Generations*, vol 26, no 1, pp 90-8.

15   Bergmark, A. and Lundstrom, T. (2002) 'Education, practice and research: knowledge and attitudes to knowledge of Swedish social workers', *Social Work Education*, vol 21, no 3, pp 359-73.

16   Berman, Y. (1995) 'Knowledge transfer in social work', *International Information and Library Review*, vol 27, no 2, pp 143-54.

[17] Biegel, D.E., Kola, L.A., Ronis, R.J., Boyle, P.E., Delos Reyes, C.M., Weider, B. and Kubek, P. (2003) 'The Ohio Substance Abuse and Mental Illness Coordinating Center of Excellence', *Research on Social Work Practice*, vol 13, no 4, pp 531-45.

[18] Blumenfield, S. and Epstein, I. (2001) 'Induction: promoting and maintaining a reflective professional staff in a hospital-based social work department', *Social Work in Health Care*, vol 33, nos 3/4, pp 1-13.

[19] Boaz, A. and Hayden, C. (2002) 'Pro-active evaluators: enabling research to be useful, usable and used', *Evaluation*, vol 8, no 4, pp 440-53.

[20] Bogenschneider, K., Olson, J.R., Linney, K.D. and Mills, J. (2000) 'Connecting research and policymaking: implications for theory and practice from the Family Impact Seminars', *Family Relations*, vol 49, pp 327-39.

[21] Brand, D. (2000) 'Practice guidance', *Professional Social Work*, vol 12.

[22] Briar, S. (1992) 'Integration of practice and research: past, present, and future', in A.J. Grasso and I. Epstein, *Research utilization in the social services: Innovations for practice and administration*, New York, NY: The Haworth Press.

[23] Bullock, R., Gooch, D., Little, M. and Mount, K. (1998) *Research in practice: Experiments in development and information design*, Aldershot: Ashgate. (**B1, B2**)

[24] Card, J.J. (2001) 'The sociometrics program archives: promoting the dissemination of evidence-based practices through replication kits', *Research on Social Work Practice*, vol 11, no 4, pp 521-6.

[25] Carr, S. (2000) 'Scottish gateway to research in social work and social care', *Noticeboard*, Spring, pp 9-10 (www.researchweb.org.uk).

[26] Catan, L. (2002) 'Making research useful', *Youth and Policy*, vol 76, pp 1-14.

[27] Charleston, G. (2001) 'Evidence-based care for carers – what do we mean?', *Journal of Dementia Care*, vol 9, no 5, pp 34-6.

[28] Cheetham, J. (2000) 'The importance of research in the education of care professionals', in R. Pierce and J. Weinstein, *Innovative education and training for care professionals*, London: Jessica Kingsley Publishers.

[29] Cheetham, J., Fuller, R., McIvor, G. and Petch, A. (1992) 'Disseminating the results of research', *Evaluating social work effectiveness*, Buckingham: Open University Press, pp 119-31.

[30] Cleaver, H., Wattam, C. and Cawson, P. (1998) *Children living at home: The initial child protection enquiry; Ten pitfalls and how to avoid them; What research tell us/Assessing risk in child protection*, London: NSPCC. (**C4**)

[31] Cornwell, N. (1992) 'From understanding to taking action: developing and assessing anti-racist/anti-discriminatory practice', *Issues in Social Work Education*, vol 12, no 2, pp 89-110.

[32] Cottrell, D. (2002) 'Body of evidence', *Young Minds Magazine*, vol 58, pp 34-7.

[33] Cox, L.E. and Burdick, D.C. (2001) 'Integrating research projects into field work experiences: enhanced training for undergraduate geriatric social work students', *Educational Gerontology*, vol 27, no 7, pp 597-608.

[34] Communities that Care (1997) *Communities that Care (UK): A new kind of prevention programme*, London: Communities that Care (UK).

[35] Dahler-Larsen, P. (2000) 'Surviving the routinization of evaluation: the administrative use of evaluations in Danish municipalities', *Administration and Society*, vol 32, no 1, pp 70-92.

[36] Daro, D. (2000) 'Linking research to practice', *Journal of Aggression, Maltreatment and Trauma*, vol 4, no 1, 7, pp 115-37.

[37] Davies, C. (1994) *A wider strategy for research and development relating to personal social services: Report to the Director of Research and Development, Department of Health, by an Independent Review Group*, London: HMSO. (**C1**)

[38] DePoy, E., Hartman, A. and Haslett, D. (1999) 'Critical action research: a model for social work knowing', *Social Work*, vol 44, no 6, pp 560-9.

[39] Dixon, L., McFarlane, W.R., Lefley, H., Luckstead, A., Cohen, M., Falloon, I., Mueser, K., Miklowitz, D., Solomon, P. and Sondheimer, D. (2001) 'Evidence-based practices for services to families of people with psychiatric disabilities', *Psychiatric Services*, vol 52, no 7, pp 903-10.

[40] Edwards, A. (2000) 'Research and practice: is there a dialogue?', in H. Penn, *Early childhood services: Theory, policy and practice*, Buckingham: Open University Press. (**C9**)

[41] Ennis, E. and Baldwin, N. (2000) 'Lifelong learning for care professionals', in R. Pierce and J. Weinstein, *Innovative education and training for care professionals*, London: Jessica Kingsley Publishers.

[42] Feinstein, O.N. (2002) 'Use of evaluations and the evaluation of their use', *Evaluation*, vol 8, no 4, pp 433-9.

[43] Feldman, P.H., Nadash, P. and Gursen, M. (2001) 'Improving communication between researchers and policy makers in long-term care: or, researchers are from Mars; policy makers are from Venus', *Gerontologist*, vol 41, no 3, pp 312-21.

[44] Fisher, T. (1997) 'Learning about child protection', *Social Work Education*, vol 16, no 2, pp 92-112. (**B11**)

45   Fuller, R. (1999) 'Practitioner research: toward reflective practice?', in M. Potocky-Tripodi and T. Tripodi, *New directions for social work practice research*, Washington, DC: National Association of Social Workers Press.

46   Gabbay, J., le May, A., Jefferson, H., Webb, D., Lovelock, R., Powell, J. and Lathlean, J. (2003) 'A case study of knowledge management in multi-agency consumer-informed "communities of practice": implications for evidence-based policy development in health and social services', *Health: An Interdisciplinary Journal for the Social Study of Health, Illness and Medicine*, vol 7, no 3, pp 283-310. (**A6**)

47   Gambrill, E. (1999) 'Evidence-based practice: an alternative to authority based practice', *Families in Society*, vol 80, no 4, pp 341-50.

48   Gambrill, E. (2001) 'Social work: an authority-based profession', *Research on Social Work Practice*, vol 11, no 2, pp 166-75.

49   Gambrill, E. (2003) 'Evidence-based practice: sea change or the emperor's new clothes?', *Journal of Social Work Education*, vol 39, no 1, pp 3-26.

50   Gibbs, L. and Gambrill, E. (2002) 'Evidence-based practice', *Research on Social Work Practice*, vol 12, no 3, p 452.

51   Ginsburg, M.B. and Gorostiaga, J.M. (2001) 'Relationships between theorists/researchers and policy makers/practitioners: rethinking the two-cultures thesis and the possibility of dialogue', *Comparative Education Review*, vol 45, no 2, pp 173-96.

52   Gomm, R. (2000) 'Would it work here?', in R. Gomm and C. Davies, *Using evidence in health and social care*, London: Sage Publications.

53   Gomm, R. (2001) 'Using what you've got for evidence based practice', Promoting the Research Friendly Workplace (workshop), Hove Town Hall, Norton Road, Hove, 6 June.

54   Grasso, A.J. (1992) 'Conclusion – information utilization: a decade of practice', in A.J. Grasso and I. Epstein, *Research utilization in the social services: Innovations for practice and administration*, New York, NY: The Haworth Press.

55   Grasso, A.J., Epstein, I. and Tripodi, T. (1988) 'Agency-based research utilization in a residential child care setting', *Administration in Social Work*, vol 12, no 4, pp 61-80.

56   Hansson, J.-H. and Haluk, S. (2003) 'Evidently sensible', *Community Care*, March, p 43.

57   Hart, E. and Bond, M. (1995) *Action research for health and social care: A guide to practice*, Buckingham: Open University Press.

58   Hart, E. and Bond, M. (2000) 'Using action research', in R. Gomm and C. Davies, *Using evidence in health and social care*, London: Sage Publications.

59   Hasenfeld, Y. and Patti, R. (1992) 'The utilization of research in administrative practice', in A.J. Grasso and I. Epstein, *Research utilization in the social services: Innovations for practice and administration*, New York, NY: The Haworth Press.

60   Healy, K. (2001) 'Participatory action research and social work: a critical appraisal', *International Social Work*, vol 44, no 1, pp 93-105.

61   Herie, M. (2002) 'Knowledge diffusion in social work: a new approach to bridging the gap', *Social Work*, vol 47, no 1, pp 85-95.

62   Hess, D. (2000) 'Working towards an evidence-based culture', *CEBSS Newsletter*, vol 7, pp 2-4.

63   Hicks, L. and Archer, L. (1998) 'Developing research mindedness in organisations', *Issues in Social Work Education*, vol 18, no 2, pp 49-54.

64   Hills, M. and Mullett, J. (2000) 'Community-based research: creating evidence-based practice for health and social change', Qualitative Evidence-based Practice Conference, Coventry University, 15-17 May.

65   Hinds, D. (2000) 'Measures, process or outcome: developing a new vocabulary to generate practice-based narratives – applying qualitative outcomes to practice', Qualitative Evidence-based Practice Conference, Coventry University, 15-17 May.

66   Hodson, R. (2003) *Leading the drive for evidence based practice in services for children and families*, RiP. (**A2**)

67   Hodson, R. and Pitt, S. (2000) 'A matter of evidence', *MCC: Building Knowledge for Integrated Care*, vol 8, no 2, pp 3-8.

68   Howard, M. and Jeffrey, J. (1999) 'Clinical practice guidelines', *Research on Social Work Practice*, vol 9, no 3, pp 283-301.

69   Howard, M.O. and Jenson, J.M. (1999) 'Barriers to development, utilization, and evaluation of social work practice guidelines', *Research on Social Work Practice*, vol 9, no 3, pp 347-64.

70   Hughes, M., McNeish, D., Newman, T., Roberts, H. and Sachdev, D. (2000) *What works? Making connections: Linking research and practice*, Ilford: Barnardo's, p 107. (**B9, B10**)

71   Humphreys, C., Berridge, D., Butler, I. and Ruddick, R. (2003) 'Making Research Count: the development of "knowledge-based practice"', *Research Policy and Planning*, vol 21, no 1, pp 41-50.

72   Humphreys, C. and Metcalfe, F. (2000) 'Research approaches for practitioners: the role of action research. What works as evidence for practice? The methodological repertoire in an applied discipline', ESRC-funded Theorising Social Work seminar paper, Cardiff, 24 May. (**C3**)

73 Hutchinson, J.R. (1995) 'A multimethod analysis of knowledge use in social policy', *Science Communication*, vol 17, no 1, pp 90-106.

74 Iwaniec, D. and McCrystal, P. (1999) 'The Centre for Child Care Research at the Queen's University of Belfast', *Research on Social Work Practice*, vol 9, no 2, pp 248-60.

75 Johnston, J. (2001) 'Evaluating national initiatives: the case of On Track', *Children and Society*, vol 15, no 1, pp 33-6.

76 Jones, J.E., Gutman, M.A. and Kaufman, N.J. (1999) 'Free to grow: translating substance abuse research and theory into preventive practice in a National Head Start Initiative', *Journal of Primary Prevention*, vol 19, no 4, pp 279-96.

77 Kahan, B. (1988) 'New directions in child care', *Children & Society*, vol 2, no 2, pp 127-37.

78 Keating, N.C., Fast, J.E., Connidis, I.A., Penning, M. and Keefe, J. (1997) 'Bridging policy and research on eldercare', *Canadian Journal on Aging*, vol 23 (Suppl), pp 22-41.

79 Keddie, D. (2002) 'Children's services in Dorset: incorporating evidence-based practice', *MCC: Building Knowledge for Integrated Care*, vol 10, no 4, pp 35-8.

80 Kelly, L., Regan, L. and Burton, S. (1998) 'Making connections – building bridges: research into action – ten years of the Child and Woman Abuse Studies Unit', *British Journal of Social Work*, vol 28, pp 601-13.

81 Kirk, S.A. (1999) 'Good intentions are not enough: practice guidelines for social work', *Research on Social Work Practice*, vol 9, no 3, pp 302-10.

82 Kirk, S.A. and Penka, C.E. (1992) 'Research utilization and MSW education: a decade of progress?', in A.J. Grasso and I. Epstein, *Research utilization in the social services: Innovations for practice and administration*, New York, NY: The Haworth Press.

83 Kirk, S.A. and Reid, W.J. (2002) *Science and social work: A critical appraisal*, Chichester: Columbia University Press.

84 Landry, R., Amara, N. and Lamari, M. (2001) 'Utilization of social science research knowledge in Canada', *Research Policy*, vol 30, no 2, pp 333-49.

85 Landry, R., Amara, N. and Lamari, N. (2001) 'Climbing the ladder of research utilization: evidence from social science research', *Science Communication*, vol 22, no 4, pp 396-422.

86 Lewis, J. (1997) 'Promoting change', *Search*, vol 28, pp 27-30.

87 Lewis, J. (1998) 'Building an evidence-based approach to social interventions', *Children & Society*, vol 12, pp 136-40.

88 Lewis, J. (2001) 'What works in community care? Evidence-based practice', *MCC: Building Knowledge for Integrated Care*, vol 9, no 1, pp 3-6.

89 Lewis, J. (2002) 'The contribution of research findings to practice change', *MCC: Building Knowledge for Integrated Care*, vol 10, no 1.

90 Little, M., Bullock, R., Madge, J. and Arruabarrena, I. (2002) 'How to develop needs-led, evidence-based services', *MCC: Building Knowledge for Integrated Care*, vol 10, no 3, pp 28-32.

91 Lomas, J. (2000) 'Connecting research and policy', *ISUMA: Canadian Journal of Policy Research*, vol 1, no 1, pp 140-4.

92 Lovell, R.D. and Turner, B.M. (1988) 'Organizational learning, bureaucratic control, preservation of form', *Knowledge: Creation, Diffusion, Utilization*, vol 9, no 3, pp 404-25.

93 Lyons, K. (2000) 'The place of research in social work education', *British Journal of Social Work*, vol 30, no 4, pp 433-47. (**C8**)

94 Macdonald, G. (1997) 'Social work research: the state we're in', *Journal of Interprofessional Care*, vol 11, no 1, pp 57-65.

95 Macdonald, G. (1998) 'Promoting evidence-based practice in child protection', *Clinical Child Psychology and Psychiatry*, vol 3, no 1, pp 71-85.

96 Macdonald, G. (1999) 'Evidence-based social care: wheels off the runway?', *Public Policy and Management*, vol 20, no 4, pp 25-32.

97 Macdonald, G. (2000) 'Social care: rhetoric and reality', in H.T.O. Davies, S.M. Nutley and P.C. Smith, *What works? Evidence-based policy and practice in public services*, Bristol: The Policy Press.

98 Macdonald, G. and Sheldon, B. (1998) 'Changing one's mind: the final frontier?', *Issues in Social Work*, vol 1, no 18, pp 3-25.

99 McCrystal, P. (2000) 'Developing the social work researcher through a practitioner research training programme', *Social Work Education*, vol 19, no 4, pp 359-73. (**C2**)

100 McWilliam, C.L. (1997) 'Using a participatory process to make a different in policy on aging', *Canadian Journal on Aging*, vol 16, no 23 (Suppl), pp 70-89.

101 Meemeduma, P. (2001) 'The corporate university and social work academic roles', *Australian Social Work*, vol 54, no 4, pp 3-12.

102 Milham, S. and Bullock, R. (1990) 'The dissemination of research findings in social work', *Department of Health Yearbook of Research and Development*, London: HMSO.

103 Miller, S.I. and Fredericks, M. (2000) 'Social science research findings and educational policy dilemmas: some additional distinctions', *Education Policy Analysis Archive*, vol 8, no 3, p 15.

104 Mitchell, C.G. (2001) 'Factors to consider in making curriculum decisions about treatment guidelines', *Journal of Social Work Education*, vol 37, no 3, pp 465-74.

105 Molas-Gallart, J., Tang, P. and Morrow, S. (2000) 'Grant funding. Assessing the non-academic impact of grant-funded socio-economic research: results from a pilot study', *Research Evaluation*, vol 9, no 3, pp 171-82. (**B14**)

106 Montieth, M. (1998) 'Developing a strategy for disseminating research findings', in D. Iwaniec and J. Pinkerton, *Making research work: Promoting child care policy and practice*, Chichester: John Wiley & Sons.

107 Moriarty, J. (2003) 'Best practice guide', *Dementia: The International Journal of Social Research and Practice*, vol 2, no 1, pp 134-5.

108 Mukherjee, S., Beresford, B, and Sloper, P. (1999) *Unlocking key working: An analysis and evaluation of key worker services for families with disabled children*, Bristol/York: The Policy Press/Joseph Rowntree Foundation.

109 Mullen, E. (1999) 'A survey of practitioner adoption and implementation of practice guidelines and evidence-based treatments', Second International Inter-Centre Network for Evaluation of Social Work Practice Conference, Stockholm. (**A10**)

110 NCDDR (National Center for the Dissemination of Disability Research) (1996) *Developing an effective dissemination plan*, Austin, TX: NCDDR.

111 NCDDR (National Center for the Dissemination of Disability Research) (1996) *Improving links between research and practice: Approaches to the effective dissemination of disability research*, Austin, TX: NCDDR.

112 NCDDR (National Center for the Dissemination of Disability Research) (1996) *Improving the usefulness of disability research: A toolbox of dissemination strategies*, Austin, TX: NCDDR.

113 NCDDR (National Center for the Dissemination of Disability Research) (1996) *A review of the literature on dissemination and knowledge utilization*, Austin, TX: NCDDR.

114 Newman, T. and McNeish, D. (2002) 'Promoting evidence based practice in a child care charity', *Social Work and Social Sciences Review*, vol 10, no 1, pp 51-62.

115 Nicholas, E. (2003) 'An outcomes focus in carer assessment and review: value and challenge', *British Journal of Social Work*, vol 33, pp 31-47. (**A12**)

116 Nutley, S.M. and Davies, H.T.O. (2000) 'Making a reality of evidence-based practice', in H.T.O. Davies, S.M. Nutley and P.C. Smith, *What works? Evidence-based policy and practice in public services*, Bristol: The Policy Press.

117   Nutley, S.M. and Davies, H.T.O. (2000) 'Making a reality of evidence-based practice: some lessons from the diffusion of innovations', *Public Policy and Management*, vol 20, no 4, pp 35-42.

118   Nutley, S.M., Davies, H.T.O. and Walter, I. (2002) *Learning from the diffusion of innovations*, St Andrews: RURU, University of St Andrews, p 29 (www.st-andrews.ac.uk/%7Eruru/publications.htm).

119   Nutley, S.M., Percy-Smith, J. and Solesbury, W. (2003) *Models of research impact: A cross-sector review of literature and practice*, London: Learning and Skills Development Agency. (**A8**)

120   Nutley, S.M., Walter, I. and Davies, H.T.O. (2003) 'From knowing to doing: a framework for understanding the evidence-into-practice agenda', *Evaluation*, vol 9, no 2, pp 125-48.

121   O'Brien, K. and Wrigton, P. (2001) 'What social workers want from research when planning for children's permanent care', *Adoption and Fostering*, vol 25, no 4, pp 68-70. (**B4**)

122   Oh, C.H. (1996) *Linking social science information to policy-making*, London: JAI Press.

123   Oh, C.H. (1997) 'Explaining the impact of policy information on policy-making', *Knowledge and Policy: The International Journal of Knowledge Transfer and Utilization*, vol 10, no 3, pp 25-55.

124   Olson, E.A. (1996) 'Evidence-based practice – a new approach to teaching the integration of research and practice in gerontology', *Educational Gerontology*, vol 22, no 6, pp 523-37.

125   OPM (Office for Public Management) (2000) *The effectiveness of different mechanisms for spreading best practice*, London: OPM, Cabinet Office. (**B8**)

126   OPM (Office for Public Management) (2003) *E2A: Understanding the transition from evidence to action in health and social care*, London: OPM.

127   Pahl, J. (1992) 'Force for change or optional extra? The impact of research on policy in social work and social welfare', in P. Carter, T. Jeffs and M.K. Smith, *Changing social work and welfare*, Buckingham: Open University Press. (**C5**)

128   Parker, J., Penhale, B., Bradley, G. and Manthorpe, J. (1998) 'The Equal Project: action research for the development of practice in dementia care', *Issues in Social Work Education*, vol 18, no 2, pp 89-96. (**B12**)

129   Penuel, W.R. and Taneekah, F. (1997) 'Participatory action research in youth programming: a theory in use', *Child and Youth Care Forum*, vol 26, no 3, pp 175-85.

130 Percy-Smith, J. with Burden, T., Darlow, A., Dawson, L., Hawtin, H. and Ladi, S. (2002) *Promoting change through research: The impact of research in local government*, York: Joseph Rowntree Foundation. (**A4**)

131 Perri 6 (2002) 'Can policy making be evidence based?', *MCC: Building Knowledge for Integrated Care*, vol 10, no 1, p 6.

132 Pierce, R. (1998) 'Promoting student and practitioner demand for social work research findings', *Issues in Social Work Education*, vol 18, no 2, pp 3-24.

133 Pinkerton, J. (1998) 'The impact of research on policy and practice: a systemic perspective', in D. Iwaniec and J. Pinkerton, *Making research work: Promoting child care policy and practice*, Chichester: John Wiley & Sons.

134 Plouffe, L.A. (2000) 'Explaining the gaps between research and policy', *ISUMA: Canadian Journal of Policy Research*, vol 1, no 1, pp 135-9.

135 Qureshi, H. and Nicholas, E. (2001) 'A new conception of social care outcomes and its practical use in assessment with older people', *Research Policy and Planning*, vol 19, no 2, pp 11-26. (**A11**)

136 Ramchandani, P., Joughin, C. and Zwi, M. (2001) 'Evidence-based child and adolescent mental health services: oxymoron or brave new dawn?', *Child Psychology and Psychiatry Review*, vol 6, no 2, pp 59-64.

137 Randall, J. (2002) 'The practice-research relationship: a case of ambivalent attachment?', *Journal of Social Work*, vol 2, no 1, pp 105-22.

138 Reid, W. (2001) 'The role of science in social work: the perennial debate', *Journal of Social Work Education*, vol 1, no 3, pp 273-93.

139 Reid, W.J. and Fortune, A.E. (1992) 'Research utilization in direct social work practice', in A.J. Grasso and I. Epstein, *Research utilization in the social services: Innovations for practice and administration*, New York, NY: The Haworth Press.

140 Richardson, A., Jackson, C. and Sykes, W. (1990) *Taking research seriously: Means of improving and assessing the use and dissemination of research*, London: HMSO. (**C6**)

141 Richardson, J., Moreland, J. and Fox, P. (2001) 'The state of evidence-based care in long-term care institutions', *Canadian Journal on Aging*, vol 20, no 3, pp 357-72. (**A9**)

142 Richey, C. and Roffman, R. (1999) 'On the sidelines of guidelines', *Research on Social Work Practice*, vol 9, no 3, pp 311-21.

143 Rickford, F. (2001) 'Make the evidence count', *Community Care*, 12 April.

144 Ring, C. (2001) 'Quality assurance in mental health-care: a case study from social work', *Health and Social Care in the Community*, vol 9, no 6, pp 383-90. (**A14**)

[145] Rose, S.D. (1992) 'Utilization of research in group work practice: an example', in A.J. Grasso and I. Epstein, *Research utilization in the social services: Innovations for practice and administration*, New York, NY: The Haworth Press.

[146] Rosen, A., Proctor, E. and Staudt, M. (1999) 'Social work research and the quest for effective practice', *Social Work Research*, vol 23, no 1, pp 4-14.

[147] Rothman, J. (1992) 'Creating tools for intervention: the convergence of research methodologies', in A.J. Grasso and I. Epstein, *Research utilization in the social services: Innovations for practice and administration*, New York, NY: The Haworth Press.

[148] Sanderson, I. (2002) 'Evaluation, policy learning and evidence-based policy making', *Public Administration*, vol 80, no 1, pp 1-22.

[149] Schoech, D., Fitch, D., MacFadden, R. and Schkade, C. (2002) 'From data to intelligence', *Administration in Social Work*, vol 26, no 1, pp 1-22.

[150] Schuerman, J., Soydan, H., Macdonald, G., Forslund, M., de Moya, D. and Boruch, R. (2002) 'The Campbell Collaboration', *Research on Social Work Practice*, vol 12, no 2, pp 309-17.

[151] Shanley, C., Lodge, M. and Mattick, R.P. (1996) 'Dissemination of research findings to alcohol and other drug practitioners', *Drug and Alcohol Review*, vol 15, no 1, pp 89-94.

[152] Sheldon, B. (1998) 'Evidence-based social services', *Research, Policy and Planning*, vol 16, no 2, pp 16-18.

[153] Sheldon, B. (2001) 'The validity of evidence-based practice in social work: a reply to Stephen Webb', *British Journal of Social Work*, vol 31, pp 801-9.

[154] Sheldon, B. and Chilvers, R. (2000) *Evidence-based social care: A study of prospects and problems*, Lyme Regis: Russell House. (**A1**)

[155] Sheldon, B. and Chilvers, R. (2002) 'An empirical study of the obstacles to evidence-based practice', *Social Work and Social Sciences Review*, vol 10, no 1, pp 6-26.

[156] Sheldon, B. and Macdonald, G. (1999) *Research and practice in social care: Mind the gap*, Bristol: CEBSS (Centre for Evidence Based Social Services)/ School for Policy Studies.

[157] Siefert, K., Jayaratne, S. and Doss Martin, L. (1992) 'Implementing the public health social work forward plan: a research-based prevention curriculum for schools of social work', *Health and Social Work*, vol 17, no 1, pp 17-27.

[158] Sinclair, R. and Jacobs, C. (1994) *Research in personal social services: The experiences of three local authorities*, London: National Children's Bureau. (**B5**)

[159] Sloper, P., Mukherjee, S., Beresford, B., Lightfoot, J. and Norris, P. (1999) *Real change not rhetoric: Putting research into practice in multi-agency services,* Bristol/York: The Policy Press/Joseph Rowntree Foundation. (**A13**)

[160] Smith, J. (1995) *Social workers as users and beneficiaries of research: A report of project funded by the ESRC,* Stirling: Social Work Research Centre, University of Stirling. (**B6**)

[161] Smith, J. and Fuller, R. (1995) 'Research links with social work practice', *Social Work Research Centre Newsletter,* vol 17, pp 4-6. (**B6**)

[162] Smyth, C., Kelly, G. and McCullough, B. (2002) *Promoting research and evidence-based practice: From rhetoric to reality,* Belfast: Northern Ireland Social Care Council.

[163] South Glamorgan Race Equality Council and South Glamorgan Social Services Department (1994) *Towards a good old age? The GOAL Project: Action research into the health,* Cardiff: South Glamorgan Race Equality Council and South Glamorgan Social Services Department.

[164] Spittlehouse, C., Acton, M. and Enock, K. (2000) 'Introducing critical appraisal skills', *Journal of Interprofessional Care,* vol 14, no 4, pp 397-404. (**B7**)

[165] Staller, K.M. and Kirk, S.A. (1998) 'Knowledge utilization in social work and legal practice', *Journal of Sociology and Social Welfare,* vol 25, no 3, pp 91-113.

[166] Stevens, L.-A. (1997) 'Action research and consultation: developing collaborative and participative relationships with communities', *Social Work,* vol 33, no 1, pp 36-43.

[167] Swinkels, A., Albarran, J.W., Means, R.I., Mitchell, T. and Stewart, M.C. (2002) 'Evidence-based practice in health and social care: where are we now?', *Journal of Interprofessional Care,* vol 16, no 4, pp 335-47.

[168] Tang, P. and Sinclair, T. (2001) 'Dissemination of results: exploitation practice in social science research', *Science and Public Policy,* vol 28, no 2, pp 131-7. (**C7**)

[169] Taylor, C. and White, S. (2001) 'Knowledge, truth and reflexivity: the problem of judgement in social work', *Journal of Social Work,* vol 1, no 1, pp 37-59.

[170] Thompson, T. and Craft, C. (2001) 'BSW students' perceptions of key competencies, values, and practitioner skills: implications for social work education', *Australian Social Work,* vol 54, no 4, pp 51-62.

[171] Torrey, W.C., Drake, R.E., Cohen, M., Fox, L.B., Lynde, D., Gorman, P. and Wyzik, P. (2002) 'The challenge of implementing and sustaining integrated dual disorders treatment programmes', *Community Mental Health Journal*, vol 38, no 6, pp 507-21.

[172] Tozer, C.L. and Ray, S. (1999) '20 questions: the research needs of children and family social workers', *Research, Policy and Planning*, vol 17, no 1, pp 7-15. (**B3**)

[173] Tripodi, T. (1992) 'Differential research utilization in macro and micro social work practice: an evolving perspective', in A.J. Grasso and I. Epstein, *Research utilization in the social services: Innovations for practice and administration*, New York, NY: The Haworth Press.

[174] Ulrich, W. (2001) 'The quest for competence in systemic research and practice', *Systems Research and Behavioral Science*, vol 18, no 1, pp 3-28.

[175] Wakefield, J.C. and Kirk, S.A. (1996) 'Unscientific thinking about scientific practice: evaluating the scientist–practitioner model', *Social Work Research*, vol 20, no 2, pp 83-95.

[176] Walter, I., Nutley, S.M. and Davies, H.T.O. (2003) *Developing a taxonomy of interventions used to increase the impact of research*, St Andrews: RURU, University of St Andrews (www.st-andrews.ac.uk/%7Eruru/publications.htm).

[177] Walter, I., Nutley, S.M. and Davies, H.T.O. (2003) *Research impact: A cross sector review*, St Andrews: RURU, University of St Andrews. (**A7**)

[178] Wambach, K.G., Haynes. D.T. and White, B.W. (1999) 'Practice guidelines: rapprochement or estrangement between social work practitioners and researchers', *Research on Social Work Practice*, vol 9, no 3, pp 322-30.

[179] Watkins, J.M. (1994) 'A postmodern critical theory of research use', *Knowledge and Policy: The International Journal of Knowledge Transfer and Utilization*, vol 7, no 4, pp 55-77.

[180] Webb, S. (2002) 'Evidence-based practice and decision analysis in social work: an implementation model', *Journal of Social Work Education*, vol 2, no 1, pp 45-63.

[181] Webb, S.A. (2001) 'Some considerations on the validity of evidence-based practice in social work', *British Journal of Social Work*, vol 31, no 1, pp 57-79.

[182] Webber, D.J. (1986) 'Explaining policymakers' use of policy information', *Knowledge: Creation, Diffusion, Utilization*, vol 7, no 3, pp 249-90.

[183] Webber, D.J. (1991) 'The distribution and use of policy knowledge in the policy process', *Knowledge and Policy: The International Journal of Knowledge Transfer and Utilization*, vol 4, no 4, pp 6-35.

184 Weiss, C.H. (1980) 'Knowledge creep and decision accretion', *Knowledge: Creation, Diffusion, Utilization*, vol 1, no 3, pp 381-404.

185 Weiss, C.H. (1987) 'The circuitry of enlightenment', *Knowledge: Creation, Diffusion, Utilization*, vol 8, no 2, pp 274-81.

186 Weiss, C.H. (1995) 'The haphazard connection', *International Journal of Educational Research*, vol 23, no 2, pp 137-50.

187 Weiss, C.H. (1998) 'Have we learned anything new about the use of evaluation?', *American Journal of Evaluation*, vol 19, no 1, pp 21-33.

188 Weyts, A., Morpeth, L. and Bullock, R. (2000) 'Department of Health Research Overviews – past, present and future: an evaluation of the dissemination of the Blue Book, "Child protection: Messages from the research"', *Child and Family Social Work*, vol 5, pp 215-23. (**A5**)

189 Whiteford, L.M. and Whiteford, V.J. (1997) 'Pregnancy and addiction: translating research into practice', *Social Science and Medicine*, vol 44, no 9, pp 1371-80.

190 Williams, J.B.W. and Lanigan, J. (1999) 'Practice guidelines in social work', *Research on Social Work Practice*, vol 9, no 3, pp 338-42.

191 Wisker, G., Tiley, J., Watkins, M., Waller, S., Thomas, J. and Wisker, A. (2001) 'Discipline-based research into student learning in English, law, social work, computer skills for linguists, women's studies, creative writing: how can it inform our teaching?', *Innovations in Education and Training International*, vol 38, no 2, pp 183-202.

192 Young, K., Ashby, D., Boaz, A. and Grayson, L. (2002) 'Social science and the evidence-based policy movement', *Social Policy and Society*, vol 1, no 3, pp 215-24.

193 Harden, A., Weston, R. and Oakley, A. (1999) *A review of the effectiveness and appropriateness of peer-delivered health promotion interventions for young people*, EPPI Research Report, London: EPPI Centre, Institute of Education, University of London (http://eppi.ioe.ac.uk/EPPIWeb/home.aspx).

194 Sackett, D.L., Rosenberg, W.M.C., Gray, J.A.M., Haynes, R.B. and Richardson, W.S. (1996) 'Evidence based medicine: what it is and what it isn't', *British Medical Journal*, vol 312, no 7023, pp 71-2.

195 Eborall, C. for Topss England (2003) *The state of the social care workforce in England. Summary of the first Annual Report of the Topss England Workforce Intelligence Unit*, Topss England.

196 DH (Department of Health) (2001) *The expert patient: A new approach to chronic disease management for the 21st century*, London: DH.

197 Chalmers, I. (1995) 'What do I want from health research and researchers when I am a patient?', *British Medical Journal*, vol 310, pp 1315-18.

[198] Attwood, M., Pedler, M., Pritchard, S. and Wilkinson, D. (2003) *Leading change: A guide to whole systems working*, Bristol: The Policy Press.

[199] Boaz, A., Ashby, D. and Young, K. (2002) *Systematic reviews: What have they got to offer evidence based policy and practice?*, ESRC UK Centre for Evidence-based Policy and Practice Working Paper 2, London: Queen Mary, University of London.

[200] Sandelowski, M. and Barroso, J. (2003) 'Classifying the findings in qualitative studies', *Qualitative Health Research*, vol 13, no 7, pp 905-23.

[201] Roberts, K.A., Dixon-Woods, M., Fitzpatrick, R., Abrams, K.R. and Jones, D.R. (2002) 'Factors affecting uptake of childhood immunisation: a Bayesian synthesis of qualitative and quantitative evidence', *Lancet*, vol 360, pp 1596-9.

[202] Crombie, I.K. (1996) *The pocket guide to critical appraisal*, London: BMJ Publishing Group.

[203] Black, T.R. (1993) *Evaluating social science research: An introduction*, London: Sage Publications.

[204] Greenhalgh, T. (1997) *How to read a paper: The basics of evidence based medicine*, London: BMJ Publishing Group.

APPENDIX 1:

Literature review methods

The literature review focused on research use within the UK social care sector. It examined empirical studies of the use of research and of the effectiveness of different methods for promoting research use as well as discussion papers about research utilisation. The review adopted a number of systematic methods to ensure transparency and rigour[199]:

- a well-defined search strategy;
- clear selection criteria for papers;
- a systematic approach to extracting data;
- quality assessment criteria for judging empirical studies;
- independent selection of papers, data extraction and quality assessment for 10% of retrievals.

The literature review was guided by the five main objectives of the knowledge review.

Search strategy

A wide range of database sources was searched, including:

- specialist databases, for example, RURU's own cross-sector database of research use papers, SIGLE (for grey literature), AgeInfo and ChildData;
- general social care databases, for example, CareData, Social Services Abstracts;
- general social science databases, for example, ASSIA (Applied Social Science Index and Abstracts), Sociological Abstracts, IBSS;
- public sector databases, for example, PAIS (Public Affairs Information Service), Planex;
- databases in related sectors, for example, MEDLINE, ERIC, BEI (British Education Index);

- general and cross-sector databases, for example, Regard, Web of Science, Article First, Cochrane Library.

A single sweep of these databases was conducted. The volume of literature returned meant that there was no scope within the current project to carry out more focused searches based on findings from the first round of searching.

A wide range of websites was also searched, including:

- websites of key social care agencies and organisations involved in promoting research use, for example, Barnardo's, RiP, MRC, CEBSS, JRF;
- key social care websites, for example, National Association of Social Workers, Council on Social Work Education, Care and Health, Society for Social Work and Research;
- research websites, for example, ESRC, Hadley Centre for Adoption and Foster Care Studies.

Trial searches did not identify any key journals suitable for hand searching. However, some additional papers were obtained through personal contacts and in conducting the fieldwork seminars.

Searches were confined to English language papers due to limited resources for translation, and to papers dating back to 1980. They focused on the UK context but wider searches on broad-based databases were also made. Searches used combinations of free text terms as the research use field is poorly indexed and difficult to search. Search terms were guided by the review objectives. The full search strategy is provided in Appendix 6. In total over 3,000 references were retrieved. All searches were documented and the results retained in Endnote libraries where possible.

To access more of the relevant 'grey' literature, we also sent a letter to all UK Directors of Social Services requesting copies of any internal reports relating to understanding and/or promoting research use. We excluded Scotland as this does not fall within SCIE's remit. Documents were received from 22 SSDs in all. These papers were handled separately from those obtained by other searches (see below).

Selection criteria

A two-stage process was used to select papers for the review. Initial broad selection criteria were used with the titles and abstracts of papers retrieved from searches (see below). Where there was any doubt as to inclusion at this stage, the full text was retrieved.

Selection criteria for papers: titles and abstracts

- Refers to research utilisation or to promoting or implementing research-based/informed policy or practice

AND
- is located within the social care sector

OR
- is a cross-sector paper that includes social care settings

OR
- is a generic paper not clearly located in any specific sector.

Full texts of papers selected at the title and abstract stage were then obtained and more detailed selection criteria applied. Different criteria were applied to the three different types of paper we aimed to include:

- empirical papers: where clear findings from empirical studies are reported;
- conceptual papers: where there is explicit development of key theories, models or frameworks for understanding;
- example papers: giving substantial detail about the form or development of initiatives to promote research use.

These criteria provided a basis for categorising papers, as empirical, conceptual or example papers. There was often overlap between categories within a single paper: for example, empirical papers sometimes also contained conceptual discussion. Appendix 2 provides more details about the content of papers.

Selection criteria: empirical papers

Report findings from empirical studies of:·

- the use of research within social care;
- the barriers to and facilitators of research use in social care;
- interventions designed to promote research use;
- defining and measuring research use;
  or
- reviews including any of the above.

Papers will be excluded where:

- research use is not a primary focus of the study;
- the study is concerned with implementing forms of data other than findings from research, for example performance monitoring data.

Selection criteria: conceptual papers

Included papers will:·

- develop or review a set of ideas about
  › implementing research-based/informed policy or practice within social care, or a sub-sector of social care;
  › defining or measuring the use of research;
  › integrating research with other types of knowledge;
  › the nature of research use (for example, the balance between replication and innovation);
  › barriers to and facilitators of research use;
- develop a clear model or conceptual framework of the process of research utilisation;
- discuss the theory used to guide a practical strategy to promote research utilisation.

Selection criteria: example papers

Included papers will:

* describe, but not evaluate, an intervention designed to promote research use.

The selection criteria were piloted on a sample of papers and slightly refined. The main areas of doubt in selecting papers occurred in defining the boundary between health and social care. We selected papers that covered settings within which social care staff work, including home care, residential care for older people and adults, fieldwork with families, adults and young people, residential care and fostering for children and independent living for disabled people. Where doubts remained about particular papers, the advice of SCIE was sought.

In total, 191 papers were selected as relevant to the review (see flowchart overleaf for more detailed breakdown). Further details of these papers are also given in Appendix 2.

Data extraction

Basic data were extracted from all papers using an Excel spreadsheet. This was used to collect details for providing a map of the literature retrieved (see Appendix 2). Basic data extracted included bibliographic details; type and content of the paper; its source and sector; whether the paper was primarily concerned with the use of research in policy or practice, or both; the main issue or research question addressed; the settings and nature of any studies reported; the nature of any interventions to promote research use described in the paper; and key discussions within conceptual papers.

Resource and time constraints meant that it was not feasible to extract in-depth data from all the studies reported in the 62 empirical papers. We decided to examine in depth only those studies conducted within UK social care settings, and reviews of such studies. The original focus of the review was on UK contexts, and additionally our reading of the non-UK studies suggested their results would not add usefully to the findings of our review. Most such studies investigated similar questions

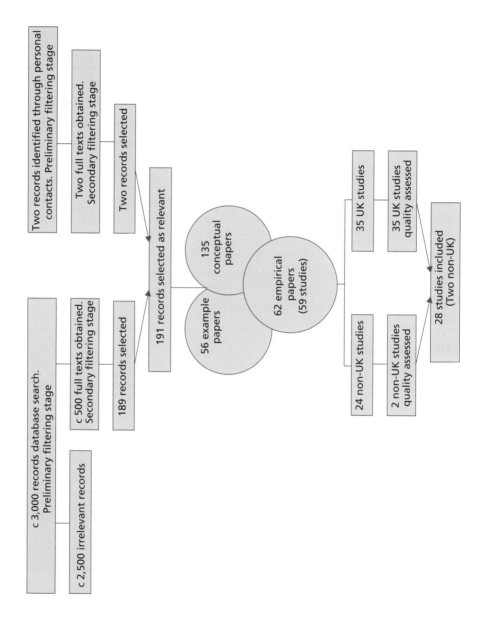

to those undertaken within UK social care settings, but raised additional issues about the transferability of their findings to UK contexts. In some cases quality issues were a concern. However, we also examined in depth two non-UK studies that examined a topic not covered by the UK studies: the use of guidelines in social care.

In-depth data were extracted from the 37 empirical studies thereby identified (see Appendix 5), again using an Excel spreadsheet. This extracted details of the research question, methods, sample, theoretical frameworks used, any research use initiative studied and the main findings. A summary of the quality assessment of the study and of the measures used to assess research use were also added in to this spreadsheet.

For conceptual papers, an outline of the key arguments and models was tabulated under the main headings of:

• implementing research-informed policy/practice within social care;
• defining/measuring research use;
• models of the research use process;
• barriers and enablers to developing research-informed policy/practice;
• integrating research knowledge with other knowledge types;
• types of research use.

A data saturation approach was taken to extracting data from conceptual papers. Where a line of argument or model appeared more than once across separate papers, this was recorded but no further details were taken.

For example papers, details of the initiatives to promote research use were tabulated together with a categorisation of the type of initiative described, for example, written materials or staff development and training.

Quality assessment

We quality assessed the evidence reported in the 37 empirical studies from which data were extracted. Checklists of quality assessment criteria were developed for and applied to different research methods used. This process is described in more detail, and the checklists themselves are provided, in Appendix 4.

The quality assessment criteria aimed to provide a framework within which to judge the validity and reliability of the results presented. However, we found evidence from the 37 studies to be of widely varying quality. We thus redefined some of our quality criteria as 'essential'. Where studies met all essential quality criteria, they were designated as good quality (category A) studies ($n=14$). Where they met at least half of these, studies were designated as less robust (category B) studies ($n=14$). Where fewer than half of the essential criteria were met, findings from these studies were not reported or synthesised in the review (category C studies, $n=9$). Studies most often failed to meet our essential quality criteria due to limited reporting of methods and data, rather than because of clear indication of poor conduct. Again, Appendix 4 provides further details.

Independent checks

An independent assessor carried out the processes of selecting papers, extracting data and quality assessment for a 10% sample of papers. Levels of agreement were high for each stage of the process, and where differences arose they were readily resolved through discussion.

Handling literature received from SSDs

A wide range of different types of document were received in response to our request to Directors of SSDs. These ranged from descriptions of current activities to promote research use to examples of policy and strategy documents that explicitly referenced research. There were no detailed evaluations of initiatives to promote research use or of studies of staff use of research. Given this, we treated these documents in a similar way to example papers. Different activities to promote research use were collated under the same categories, and details of initiatives were recorded. We also noted the ways in which research had been used by SSDs by examining how research had been referenced in policy and other documents that we received.

Synthesis of findings

The varied nature of the data located by the review meant that it was not possible to aggregate them through established quantitative or qualitative approaches to synthesis, such as meta-analysis or meta-ethnography. Despite this, we aimed to use rigorous methods for synthesising results from different sources. In addition, empirical studies from the literature were quality assessed before any synthesis of their findings was conducted, and findings from those judged to be poor quality (C-rated studies) were excluded from the synthesis process.

Because the data located by the review were so varied, our focus in extracting data was on findings: the judgements or discoveries made by the original researchers on the basis of the data reported, rather than the raw data themselves. This approach has been used in relation to qualitative data[200] but we found that it could be applied to quantitative data as well. For each study identified in the literature, and for the seminars and interviews, findings were extracted according to the following questions:

1. How is research conceptualised in relation to its use?
2. How is research used?
3. What are the barriers/enablers to research use?
4. How is research use promoted?
5. How effective are different methods of promoting research use?
6. What are the barriers/enablers to different methods of promoting research use?

These questions were agreed within the team after initial piloting and aimed to reflect the main objectives of the review. Findings were extracted using the original researchers' own terms and categories.

Members of the review team then shared the different sets of findings from the literature review and from the fieldwork and independently identified themes within and across them. We focused on identifying themes from the findings because the nature of the data we had extracted meant that no quantitative aggregation of findings was possible. Our approach was akin to that of the conceptual coding process involved in a grounded qualitative analysis. Other studies have also identified key categories from across both quantitative and qualitative findings in developing a method for meta-analysis[201]. We aimed to identify key issues or concepts that recurred within different sets of findings. These were then discussed at a team meeting, and the themes were agreed on as a group. This ensured that they were grounded in the original findings and were clearly identifiable by more than one researcher. Themes were developed independently for findings from category A and category B studies, but no theme was identified in findings from the less robust studies that had not already been identified within the better quality findings.

To identify models of research use in social care, we drew on two sources of data:

- the themes identified across different sets of findings;
- the different practices to promote research use in social care that occurred in the literature, fieldwork and SSD documentation.

Members of the team drew up lists of all the practices used to promote research use identified in each of these sources. As a team, we then categorised the practices according to whether they were undertaken by:

- researchers;
- practitioners or practice managers;
- practice-based intermediaries such as local research/practice posts; or
- intermediary organisations:
  - whose primary role is to support the use of research, such as CEBSS, MRC and SCIE, or
  - for whom supporting research use is a secondary role, such as Barnardo's, professional organisations, government departments or the SSI.

These four new lists, developed on flip charts, were then examined alongside the themes we had identified in order to locate further categories, patterns, assumptions and processes within these sources. This analysis took place as a team, through debating and refining our ideas. Once we thought that we had identified a coherent 'model' of research use, we wrote down its key features, again on a flip chart, and checked and re-checked our thinking against our themes and our lists of practices. We also debated the content of each model, and the ideas underlying it, in an active, iterative and challenging process. When we felt we had identified the key models of research use in this way, we went back to our lists of practices and our themes to check for any contradictory findings, and to ensure that our models fully covered them all. Our approach was thus inductive: we aimed to develop our models in a 'bottom-up' way, starting with the review's findings and what was happening on the ground in social care, rather than starting with existing conceptual models and attempting to find evidence that reflected or contradicted them.

Once we had developed the models, we returned to the individually extracted findings in order to locate any evidence about:

- the likely effectiveness of the models' approaches to developing research use in social care;
- any barriers or enablers to developing the models.

Where studies reported similar findings, these were straightforwardly collated in presenting the evidence within the report, using a narrative rather than quantitative approach. This approach aimed to preserve the results of different studies within their original contexts.

APPENDIX 2:

Map of the literature

This appendix presents a map of the literature included in the review. It gives an indication of the nature of evidence about research use in the social care field more generally. The specific studies providing evidence to support the review's findings are detailed in Appendix 5. The map excludes documents received from SSDs, which were handled separately (see Appendix 1). It should be noted that the nature of the papers retrieved will reflect the focus of our search strategy on database sources.

Key details of all 191 full text papers selected as relevant to the review were entered onto an Excel spreadsheet (see Appendix 1). These details form the basis of the mapping exercise that follows which looks at the source, type and content of all selected papers.

All but two papers were located through database searches. The remaining two were identified from personal contacts. Website searches returned no papers that met the selection criteria for the review, but RURU conducted extensive searches of key websites in the summer of 2002 and any returns from these would have been identified through the RURU database. The RURU database itself accounted for 36% of included papers, and CareData a further 27%.

Nearly three quarters of selected papers are journal articles. Fourteen per cent are book chapters or books, and 10% are published reports. The remainder are conference papers and online reports. Only six papers date from before 1990, and over 100 date from 2000 or later. This may reflect both the content of databases searched, and also the current interest in the evidence-informed policy and practice agenda.

In terms of content:

- 62 papers report findings from an empirical study of the use of research in social care, or an evaluation of an initiative to promote research use (empirical papers)
  4, 8-9, 13-15, 20, 23, 30, 33, 35, 37, 40, 43-4, 46, 55, 61, 66, 70, 72-3, 82, 84-5, 93, 99, 105, 108-9, 115, 119, 121-3, 125, 127-30, 135, 140-1, 144, 146, 151, 154-5, 157-61, 164, 168, 170, 172, 177, 182, 184, 188-9

- 56 describe but do not evaluate an initiative to promote research use (example papers)
  2, 7, 10, 12, 17-19, 21, 23-6, 29, 31, 34, 36-8, 45, 56, 62-3, 65, 67, 71, 74-6, 79-80, 86, 90, 93, 100, 102, 107, 110, 114, 121, 124-7, 132, 134, 137, 140, 143, 145, 149-50, 154, 163, 171, 188, 191

- 135 contain some conceptual discussion (conceptual papers
  3-6, 8-9, 11-12, 16, 18-20, 22-3, 26-9, 32, 35, 37-42, 44, 46-55, 57-61, 64-6, 68-72, 77-8, 81, 83-9, 91-2, 94-9, 101, 103-6, 111-14, 116-20, 122-5, 127-34, 136-40, 142, 146-9, 151-6, 159, 162, 165-7, 169-70, 173-88, 190, 192

Clearly there is overlap in content: for example, more than half of empirical papers also had some conceptual content. However, 43% of all papers were solely conceptual in content.

Two thirds of papers came from the social care sector, and a further quarter were cross-sector papers that included social care settings or looked at the use of social research in general. Most of the remainder covered both health and social care settings. The majority (125 papers) examined the use of research by practitioners, and a further 45 papers looked jointly at the use of research in policy and practice. Only 21 papers looked solely at the use of research in policy making.

Empirical papers

The 62 empirical papers reported a total of 59 studies*. Of these:

- 23 were *studies of initiatives* to promote research use in a social care or multidisciplinary sector, of which 15 were in UK settings
  8-9, 20, 23, 30, 33, 40, 46, 61, 72, 99, 108, 115, 127-9, 135, 144, 151, 157, 159, 164, 188, 189

- 31 were *studies of the use of research* by practitioners and/or policy makers, their attitudes to research, or the barriers and enablers to using research, of which 16 were in UK settings
  4, 13, 15, 23, 35, 37, 43-4, 55, 66, 70, 73, 82, 84-5, 93, 105, 121-3, 130, 140, 146, 153-4, 158, 160-1, 168, 170, 172, 182, 184

- 5 were reviews of such studies (of which one was oriented to non-UK settings
  14, 70, 119, 125, 177

Note: *It should be noted that in some instances, more than one study/review was reported in a single paper, and some studies were reported in more than one paper.

Only one of the *studies of initiatives* to promote research use employed an experimental approach to assess effectiveness. Other studies report outcome and/or process findings from evaluations. They use a range of methods but usually rely on self-report measures of effectiveness gathered through questionnaire surveys, evaluation forms and interviews.

All but four of the initiatives studied aimed to encourage research use by practitioners rather than policy makers. Most studies from outside the UK were based in the US and Canada. The majority were located in social care settings, including adult and children's services and social work education. A wide range of participants were involved in these studies, including professional social workers, wider social care staff, researchers, policy makers and service users.

A range of different interventions to promote research use were studied (see below).

Types of intervention studied

Intervention type	Number of studies
Action research	7
Staff training or support for implementing research-based practice tools	4
Conferences/seminars/workshops plus distribution of written materials	4
Social work education	3
Implementing research-based services or interventions	2
Provision of expert support in using research	1
Critical appraisal skills training	1
Distribution of written materials	1
Total	**23**

Of the 31 *studies of the use of research* by practitioners and/or policy makers, nearly half (15) were conducted using questionnaire surveys. Six used qualitative methods, and the remainder used a mix of approaches. Studies of practitioners' use of research primarily examined professionally qualified social workers or those training as social workers. A range of settings were represented, including long-term care, mental health and children and families, and local and national level policy making.

Nature of the empirical evidence

All 37 empirical studies selected as relevant to the review were quality assessed (see Appendices 1 and 4). However, some general issues about problems with and gaps within the evidence base around research use in social care also emerged:

- The review focused on evidence from UK social care settings, but sometimes findings from studies conducted in North America or across a number of different sectors within the UK are reported. While lessons can be learnt from elsewhere, care should be taken in generalising findings across different contexts. This also applies to transferring findings across different settings and staff groups within the social care sector.
- The quality of empirical studies was often not judged to be high. One of the difficulties in assessing quality was the lack of sufficient or clear information about the conduct of research. Sometimes this was apparently due to lack of space. A further problem related to reporting of findings, which were not always clearly separable from authors' discussions or the findings of other studies.
- Research is not neutral, and the nature of the evidence collected will reflect certain values and concerns. In particular, studies of the use of research by social care staff have focused on individuals reading, and then applying, research findings. As we have seen, this represents only one particular model of how research is used.
- Drawing together findings across studies fails to examine the extent of any change in research use over time. However, included studies were sometimes conducted several years apart. Change over time is difficult to assess without explicit collection of longitudinal data. Further, much activity in the sector is new, and repeat studies or evaluations of initiatives may not yet be reported.
- Defining and measuring research use typically received little attention in the studies whose findings were included in the review, although there were exceptions (for example, **B2**, **B14**). Many studies let respondents define for themselves what might be meant by the 'use'

or 'impact' of research on their practice. Few attempted more objective measures of research use (for example, **A14**; **B2**).

- The review itself has some limitations. Although a wide range of sources were searched, poor indexing of the research use field means retrievals are unlikely to be comprehensive. Further searches using reference lists of included studies may increase returns but are time- and labour-intensive. In addition, we relied on abstracts to sift papers but these are not always adequately informative in the social science literature.

Conceptual papers

The content of conceptual papers was grouped according to the following categories, derived from a conceptual map of the terrain of research use:[120]

- general models of the research use process: 80 papers;
- models or strategies for implementing research-informed policy/ practice within social care: 48 papers. These tend to focus on social workers, rather than social care more widely;
- barriers and enablers to developing research-informed policy/practice: 33 papers;
- types of research use, for example direct or indirect use of research: 26 papers;
- discussions around defining and/or measuring research use: 11 papers;
- how research knowledge is integrated with other knowledge types: 10 papers.

Some papers had content which covered more than one of these categories.

Example papers

A wide range of initiatives to promote research use were detailed in the 56 example papers identified. Eleven papers described the activities of organisations specifically developed to promote research use in social care (for example, CEBSS). Twelve detailed initiatives involved practitioners in research in different ways, such as action research or practitioner research programmes. Forms of research-based guidance, such as handbooks and guidelines, were described in four papers. Other interventions described were:

- collaborations, such as partnerships between practice organisations and universities;
- improving access to research findings;
- interactive education, such as participative workshops;
- networks for feeding research findings into policy/practice;
- planning research to meet users' needs;
- developing written materials, such as research briefings;
- staff development;
- training to support the use of research;
- multi-component initiatives, using a range of approaches to promote research use.

APPENDIX 3

Fieldwork seminars and interviews

Four consultation seminars and seven interviews were held with people in the social care field.

Both the seminars and the interviews sought to address the following key questions:

- How is research used to inform practice change and with what effect?
- How is research seen in comparison with other kinds of knowledge?
- What are the barriers to using research to change social care practice?
- Are there differences in experience across sectors/types of service?
- To what extent and how are practitioners involved in research themselves?
- What kinds of staff development, training and education processes encourage research use?
- What role can policy makers, managers and practitioners play in research use?
- What role can service users play in challenging practitioners' attitudes and behaviours on the basis of research?
- How could barriers to research use be addressed?
- How do we know what works in research use?

The consultation seminars were held in Leeds, London, Belfast and Cardiff and were attended by a total of 135 social care practitioners and educators from the voluntary and statutory sectors. A breakdown of those attending is listed overleaf.

Analysis of delegates to seminars

Statutory	
• Managers	40
• Practitioners	8
• Learning and development	25
Voluntary organisations	22
Academics	11
Intermediary organisations	16
Other	13
Total	135

Each seminar began with a presentation from the research team outlining the project and summarising existing understanding about barriers and enablers of research use in general. Participants were then invited in plenary session to comment on these barriers and enablers from the point of view of social care staff. This was followed by a round table discussion, facilitated by a member of the research team, of research utilisation initiatives that participants had initiated or participated in.

Delegates then broke into small, mixed groups to discuss actions that they felt might lead to more effective research utilisation, focusing in particular on:

• staff development, training and education;
• roles and responsibilities of managers, practitioners and policy makers;
• potential role of service users;
• differences across sector/types of service.

Each group was facilitated by a member of the research team and the discussion recorded by a note taker.

A final plenary session provided an opportunity for delegates to share any further thoughts and for the research team to request documentation relating to initiatives mentioned during the course of the seminar.

Following each seminar the note takers and facilitators produced notes of the day. These were then compared to check for accuracy of interpretation. On completion of all four seminars a summary was prepared organised along thematic lines. This was then sent to all participants with a request for comments and corrections.

In addition, seven interviews were undertaken with key personnel in the GSCC, Topss England, National Care Homes Association, UKHCA, Department of Health, Shaping Our Lives, and Wales Office of Research and Development.

The interviews were conducted face-to-face by a member of the research team using a standard discussion guide. Each interview was tape-recorded and then transcribed. The transcriptions were then thematically analysed and the additional material incorporated into a final combined report on both the seminars and interviews.

APPENDIX 4

Quality assessment of empirical studies

All 37 empirical studies selected as relevant to the review were quality assessed using checklists of criteria. These drew on quality assessment criteria developed for use with conventional research accounts (for example, [193,202,203,204]). Separate checklists were developed for use with:

- intervention studies (for example, randomised controlled trials [RCTs], quasi-experimental designs);
- surveys;
- studies using qualitative methods;
- reviews.

The checklists are reproduced in full at the end of this appendix. Each comprises some common basic quality criteria together with criteria specific to the study design in question. Where studies employed mixed methods, the different research components were assessed using more than one checklist. A brief overall summary of key quality issues was also completed.

Although explicit quality assessment criteria were used, the process of applying such criteria is always one of informed judgement. However, in order to enhance the reliability of this process, a second independent assessor applied the quality criteria to a 10% sample of empirical studies. Overall agreement between assessors about study quality for these studies was found to be high.

The quality assessment criteria were not originally intended to be used to judge whether studies should be included in the review, but were viewed as a framework within which to judge the validity and reliability of the results presented. However, in practice we found that it was sometimes very hard to assess study quality. This was usually because of lack of information about methods; or because results were not clearly reported or linked to study methods. Two of the review team thus re-examined the quality assessment criteria and drew out those criteria they felt to be:

a) essential and
b) desirable.

These are marked E and D in the checklists below.

For a study to be judged as good quality (**A1–A14**, see Appendix 5), all essential criteria had to be met. For a study to be judged as less robust (**B1–B14**), at least half of the essential criteria had to be met. Where fewer than half of the essential criteria were met, a study's results were excluded from the empirical findings reported and synthesised in the review (**C1–C9**). Overall this process of quality assessment aimed to be generous about including studies. Where studies were excluded, this was most often due to problems with reporting methods and/or findings, rather than due to an indication that a study had been poorly conducted. The annotated bibliographies of these studies in Appendix 5 provide a supplement to the quality assessment through which to judge the findings reported (for example, by giving details of sample sizes and survey response rates).

Conceptual and example papers and content were not quality assessed.

Quality assessment checklists

Quality assessment criteria: intervention studies

Aims
• Are the aims of the study clearly stated? (E)

Conceptual framework
• Is there an explicit account of the theoretical literature and/or inclusion of a literature review which demonstrates how the study is informed by or linked to an existing body of knowledge? (D)

Study design
• Is the study design appropriate to the stated aims? (E)

- Are the study design and data collection processes adequately described? (D)
- Were any comparison groups used equivalent? (E)
- Were any comparison groups treated equally aside from the intervention? (E)

Sampling
- Is the sampling strategy clearly described and justified? (E)

Results
- Are the outcome measures used sufficiently valid and reliable for the purpose of the study? (E)
- Are pre-test data reported? (D)
- Are post-test data reported? (E)
- Was follow-up of participants complete? (D)

Analysis
- Are results analysed by original group allocation? (E)
- Are the methods of analysis adequately described? (D)
- Are there obvious errors in analysis? (E, no obvious errors)

Conclusions
- Are there evident sources of bias in the results reported? (E, no evident sources of bias)

Overall summary

Quality assessment criteria: surveys

Aims
- Are the aims of the study clearly stated? (E)

Conceptual framework
- Is there an explicit account of the theoretical literature and/or inclusion of a literature review which demonstrates how the study is informed by or linked to an existing body of knowledge? (D)

Study design
- Is the study design appropriate to the stated aims? (E)
- Are the study design and data collection processes adequately described? (D)

Sampling
- Is the sampling strategy clearly described and justified? (E)
- Is the sample representative? (D)

Results
- Is the response rate adequate? (D)
- Are the measures used sufficiently valid and reliable for the purpose of the study? (E)
- Are the basic data adequately described? (D)

Analysis
- Are the methods of analysis adequately described? (D)
- Are there obvious errors in analysis? (E, no obvious errors)

Conclusions
- Are there evident sources of bias in the results reported? (E, no evident sources of bias)

Overall summary

Quality assessment criteria: studies using qualitative methods

Aims
- Are the aims of the study clearly stated? (E)

Conceptual framework
- Is there an explicit account of the theoretical literature and/or inclusion of a literature review which demonstrates how the study is informed by or linked to an existing body of knowledge? (D)

Study design
- Is the study design appropriate to the stated aims? (E)
- Are the study design and data collection processes adequately described? (D)
- Is the researcher's perspective clearly stated and taken into account? (D)

Sampling
- Is the sampling strategy clearly described and justified? (E)
- Is there a clear description of the context and participants of the study? (D)

Conclusions
- Are there evident sources of bias in the results reported? (E, no evident sources of bias)
- Is sufficient indication provided to demonstrate that the findings and conclusions are grounded in the data? (E)

Overall summary

Quality assessment criteria: reviews

Aims
- Are the aims of the review clearly stated? (E)

Sampling
- Is the search strategy for papers clearly described and justified? (E)
- Is it likely that important, relevant studies were missed in the search for papers? (D)
- Are the inclusion and exclusion criteria appropriate to the review's aims? (D)
- Was the quality of studies adequately assessed? (E)

Results
- Are the results of all studies adequately described? (D)
- Are the reasons for any heterogeneity in results considered? (D)

Synthesis
- Were efforts made to address the effects of any missing information? (D)
- Were efforts made to take into account the effects of important biases? (D)

Conclusions
- Are the findings of the review clear? (E)
- Are the main relevant outcomes considered? (E)
- Are the conclusions drawn by the review justified? (E)

Overall summary

Annotated list of studies

For the list presented below, studies are reported independently of the papers in which they appear. A total of 37 studies are detailed, which appear in 38 different papers. It should be noted that:

- for two studies (**A1** and **B6**), the same findings are reported in two different papers;
- two papers report two separate studies apiece (Bullock, 1998 – **B1**, **B2**, and Hughes, 2000 – **B9**, **B10**);
- two different sets of findings from a single study are reported in two separate papers (**A13**).

A1
Sheldon and Chilvers, 2000[154]
[also reported in Sheldon and Chilvers, 2002[155]]

Nature of study
- Large-scale survey of research access, knowledge and use among front-line professional grade social care staff in 16 local authorities.

Sample and methods
- Sixteen local authority SSDs in CEBSS.
- Forty-two-instrument questionnaire sent to representative sample of 2,285 front-line professional grade staff: social workers, occupational therapists and others, 1,226 replies used for analysis.

What was studied
- Departmental influences on the availability and use of research.
- Reading habits and preferences.
- Familiarity with research publications.
- Knowledge of research issues and terms.
- Attitudes to research-based approaches.
- Views on activities to help further CEBSS' aims.

Quality assessment

- Large-scale survey and comprehensive research instrument, albeit restricted to SSDs signed up to CEBSS.

A2

Hodson, 2003[66]

Nature of study

- Exploratory study within RiP member agencies to gauge the ability of child care agencies to lead evidence-based practice.

Sample and methods

- Delphi questionnaire sent to 60 staff in children and families services in research, policy or planning roles in six local authorities.
- Nine telephone interviews with second-tier managers, managers of front-line team managers, front-line team managers and policy/research staff from voluntary agencies and local authorities.

What was studied

- What skills, behaviours, knowledge, experience and personal qualities are needed to lead evidence-based practice.
- Barriers and opportunities to developing this leadership.
- What support may be needed to further work on developing evidence-based practice.

Quality assessment

- Results mostly derived from small-scale study but level of detail of findings presented suggests these are well grounded in original data.

A3

Barratt, 2003[13]

Nature of study

- Three-stage collaborative project by RiP examining how evidence-based practice can be supported.

Sample and methods
- Exploration of evidence-based practice by 40 agency representatives during annual two-day meeting through small group discussions.
- Telephone interviews with 36 managers from six participating agencies.
- Questionnaire comprising 110 statements derived from telephone interviews sent to 50 senior staff within the six agencies; included directors and policy, planning and quality managers: 40 responses.

What was studied
- The nature of evidence.
- Access to evidence and its dissemination.
- Overt and explicit use of evidence.
- Responsibility/accountability and team working around evidence-based practice.
- Monitoring and evaluation of evidence-based practice.
- Barriers to the development of evidence-based practice.

Quality assessment
- Robustness of findings are supported by a three-stage study process but study is limited to senior staff.

A4
Percy-Smith et al, 2002[130]

Nature of study
- Survey and case studies of local authorities' use of research to inform policy development and implementation.

Sample and methods
- Five copies of a questionnaire sent to all local authorities in England, Scotland and Wales to be distributed to five officers across a range of departments with responsibility for research or key users of research: 696 returned.
- Six case studies included:
  - at least one local authority in England, Scotland and Wales;
  - at least one Metropolitan Authority, Unitary Authority, County Council and District Council.

- Aimed to track the journey of key research reports through local authorities but proved impossible.

What was studied

- Processes and outcomes of research dissemination, use and impact in local authorities.
- The use of research to inform corporate level policy development.
- The use of research at different levels within local authorities.
- How the value and usefulness of research can be enhanced in local authorities.

Quality assessment

- Wide-ranging survey using robust instrument. Findings supported by case studies but these lack full details of methods.

A5
Weyts et al, 2000[188]

Nature of study

- Survey of the impact and use of the Department of Health 'Blue Book'.

Sample and methods

- Five hundred professionals randomly selected from databases were mailed questionnaires, a mix of social services (majority), education, police, health and voluntary sector employees in local authorities in England and Wales: 241 responses.
- One hundred professionals (similar mix) administered questionnaire by telephone: 51 responses.
- Two thirds of respondents were managers, 17% team managers, one quarter front-line staff.

What was studied

- Awareness of the Blue Book.
- Use of the Blue Book.
- Perceived impact of the Blue Book.
- Comments and suggestions as to the Blue Book's dissemination.

Nature of intervention

- The Department of Health 'Blue Book' – *Child protection: Messages from the research* – a written overview of selected research findings providing clear messages plus 'True for Us' exercises aiming to encourage professionals to evaluate their own practice and attitudes.
- High profile ministerial launch and extensive circulation of free copies plus series of regional day conferences.

Quality assessment

- Well-conducted study given practical and cost constraints.

A6

Gabbay et al, 2003[46]

Nature of study

- Observational study of attempt to feed research information into health and social care policy development through two multistakeholder 'Communities of Practice' (CoPs).

Sample and methods

- Multistakeholder CoPs, one in each of two Primary Care Groups (PCGs) comprising consumers and representatives from PCGs, community trusts/hospitals, acute trusts, social services, private and voluntary sectors, health authority and health service library.
- Research team facilitated the CoPs and non-participant observer attended and taped all meetings; used analysis to plan future meetings; research team also recorded their views in reflective diaries.
- Sixty-eight interviews with CoPs members.

What was studied

- How the CoPs acquired, negotiated and used knowledge in collective decision-making processes.

Nature of intervention

- NHS Executive South East Region Research and Development Directorate commissioned two multistakeholder CoPs to be established and facilitated to improve health/social services for the over-50s.

- Groups worked together as CoPs to formulate common policies to improve services, facilitated by two members of the research team who aimed to tread a line between allowing groups to proceed 'naturally' and pressing them too hard towards traditional evidence-based policy/practice methods.

Quality assessment
- Rigorous, well-conducted qualitative study with good reflexivity.

A7
Walter et al, 2003[177]

Nature of study
- Cross-sector literature review of approaches to enhancing the impact of research.

Sample and methods
- Literature searched through key databases in the health, education, criminal justice and social care fields, plus general databases.
- Health care papers restricted to reviews and overviews and evaluations of large-scale initiatives.
- Selection criteria used to sift papers.
- Studies were quality assessed.
- 5,800 papers scanned: 341 included, 125 empirical, of which 60% were from the health care field.
- UK focus but studies from abroad as well.

What was studied
- Models that guide research impact thinking and practice.
- The effectiveness of different approaches to enhancing the impact of research.
- How the impact of research is best assessed.

Nature of intervention
- Diverse interventions studied within the different sectors covered.

Quality assessment
- Uses systematic approach to searching and handling of papers and quality assesses studies.

A8
Nutley et al, 2003[119]

Nature of study
- National cross-sector study conducted for the Learning and Skills Development Agency on enhancing the impact of research, drawing on a literature review and case studies of organisations.

Sample and methods
- Literature review (see **A7**).
- Case studies of organisations that used, funded or produced research with local and national remits and covering a range of sectors and disciplines: JRF, Barnardo's, Local and Regional Government Research Unit (LGRU), Office of the Deputy Prime Minister (ODPM), MORI Social Research Institute, Local Government Association (LGA) – involved review of relevant documents and interviews with key actors using piloted protocol.
- Two one-day workshops with members of the regional Learning and Skills Research Networks and a Learning and Research Skills Centre colloquium, involving presentation of research followed by discussion to 'test out' findings.

What was studied
- The effectiveness of different practices for enhancing the impact of research.
- Barriers and enablers to enhancing research impact.

Quality assessment
- Broadly well-conducted study, although limited details of data collection for case studies.

A9
Richardson et al, 2001[141]

Nature of study
- Survey in Ontario, Canada of use of practice guidelines in chronic care and long-term care facilities.

Sample and methods
- 550 hospitals, nursing homes and homes for the aged in Ontario, Canada.
- Mailed questionnaire: 306 returned.

What was studied
- Awareness and use of evidence-based practice guidelines.
- Views on conditions for which guidelines might be developed in the future.
- Views on what stimulates practice change.

Nature of intervention
- Practice guidelines.

Quality assessment
- A well-conducted survey albeit within a limited geographical area.

A10
Mullen, 1999[109]

Nature of study
- Survey of professional staff in a US voluntary mental health/social service agency.

Sample and methods
- Large urban voluntary mental health/social service agency in the US.
- Five hundred staff engaged in providing clinical services, mostly social workers.
- Mailed questionnaire: 124 responses.

What was studied
- Awareness of practice guidelines.
- Nature of guidelines known about and used.
- Attitudes to the use of guidelines.
- Reading and use of research and research methods in practice.
- Preferences for guidelines based on expert consensus/research.

Quality assessment
- Well-conducted survey but of a single agency. Findings limited by low response rate but provide initial information about an unresearched area.

A11
Qureshi and Nicholas, 2001[135]

Nature of study
- Analysis of development process and trial implementation of research-based tools for assessing outcomes of care for older people.

Sample and methods
- Trial implementation involved 12 staff: 7 social worker/care managers, 2 senior practitioners and 3 home care organisers, working in hospital settings and the community.
- Thirty anonymised assessment forms and evaluative self-completion forms were returned.
- Diary sheets were also used by staff to record whether tools had changed practice.

What was studied
- Changes to the assessment, care plan and planning processes.
- Changes to the way care packages were implemented, delivered and reviewed.
- Use of the tools.
- Barriers and enablers to implementing the tools.

Nature of intervention

- Research and development project to develop a form for recording intended outcomes in assessment for older people in social care. Service users and social care staff were involved in initial research.
- Assessment form was developed through meetings between researchers and staff, including two collaborative workshops involving 17 staff who undertook assessments. Tools subsequently revised.
- Tools used in trial implementation involved two documents: an assessment summary and a prompt list.
- Twelve staff involved in trial implementation were recruited and briefed by two care managers who were on the original planning group.

Quality assessment

- Well-conducted small-scale research and development study. Some presentation of original data to support overall findings.

A12

Nicholas, 2003[115]

Nature of study

- Evaluation of trial implementation of research-based practice tools supporting an outcomes approach to assessment and review for carers of older people.

Sample and methods

- Trial implementation in one of two local authorities participating in research and development project.
- Fourteen staff across three community teams specialising in older people and one hospital team.
- Thirty-seven assessments with carers of older people: 15 were also reviewed.
- Carers identified and invited to participate in course of normal work: 22 already known and 15 new referrals.
- Written reflections by individual assessors after each assessment and review.
- Interviews with a sample of 12 carers who had been assessed.
- Interviews with all 14 staff participants.

- Analysis of completed documentation and discussion with staff and managers.

What was studied
- Staff and carers' views on use and value of outcome assessment forms.
- Impact of outcome assessment forms on practice.
- Barriers and enablers to implementing outcome assessment forms.

Nature of intervention
- Research and development project undertaken in partnership with local authority.
- Briefing and training for volunteer assessors and line managers through workshops, some of which involved carers as well.
- Outcome assessment sheets developed in the form of self-completion questionnaires: structured summary sheet enabled assessors to record and check their conclusions. Included feedback forms for carers.

Quality assessment
- Well-conducted small-scale evaluation drawing on a range of sources.

A13
Sloper et al, 1999[159]
Mukherjee et al, 1999[108]

Nature of study
- Researched development project undertaken by the JRF to implement research-based key worker services for families with disabled children in two local authority SSDs.

Part I (reported in Sloper, 1999[159])
Sample and methods
- Two local authority SSDs pilot sites.
- Multiagency steering groups which planned and managed the implementation of key worker services, included education, social services and health care staff, plus voluntary sector representation in one site and parent representation in the other.

- Multimethod, reflexive, flexible approach, included group reflection sessions for research team and site teams and individual reflections for participants.
- Researcher acted as outside observer.
- Workshop evaluation questionnaires.
- Data were also obtained from recorded minutes and field notes of researchers' meetings with site teams and minutes of other meetings.

What was studied
- The development of pilot key worker services for families with disabled children, in terms of input, process, output and change.

Nature of intervention
- Three workshops with multiagency steering groups from each site: grounded in concept of a cycle of innovation and theories of group process and planning change. Researchers aimed to provide the information and conditions to facilitate the development of key worker services in each site:
  - workshop one: initial two-day residential workshop to disseminate research information on key worker services and develop action plans;
  - workshop two: one day, held at six-month point, to reflect on experiences and develop further action plans;
  - workshop three: two-day workshop, after one year, reflected on process, drew up guidelines for other areas and prepared sites for exit of research team.
- Researchers also maintained regular contact with steering groups.
- Intervention taken forward differently at each site:
  - site 1: senior managers formed subgroup to steering group which met separately to make major decisions and took the lead in planning training. Other members of the steering group disseminated information. Managers asked individual members of staff to be key workers who then identified families. One local manager acted as coordinator for the service. Key workers had regular individual and group supervision meetings with the coordinator;
  - site 2: subgroup with representatives from all agencies designed training in consultation with the steering group. All steering group members were involved in recruiting both key workers and families

on a voluntary basis. Key workers had monthly support group meetings, and were offered mentors.

Quality assessment
- Careful and robust account paying good attention to the role of the researcher in this type of study.

Part II (reported in Mukherjee, 1999[108])
Sample and methods
- Two local authority SSDs.
- Key workers included 18 social workers, also nurses, education professionals, a health visitor, a home manager and a voluntary sector worker.
- Data from material generated during project workshops (see **A13**).
- Telephone interviews with key workers at start and end of pilot, including completion of a key worker 'activities scale'.
- Interviews with parents who also completed a key worker 'activities scale'.
- Interviews with eight managers from sub-groups of steering groups – involved representatives from health, education and social services.

What was studied
- The process and outcomes of developing and implementing research-based pilot key worker services.
- Views on the services of the families, key workers and steering groups involved.

Nature of intervention
- Site 1:
  - identified staff and families to take part in the key worker service;
  - initial one-day training event for key workers;
  - project coordinator provided regular individual supervision and support group meetings and link with steering group;
  - small-scale pilot to observe and test out model of key worker service developed.
- Site 2:
  - key workers and families recruited by volunteering which determined the size of the pilot;
  - initial one-day information event for key workers;

> ‣ steering group provided support group meetings; offer of a mentor, not taken up; a model case file; and a supervision session towards the end of the pilot.

Quality assessment
• Robust study grounded in a realist approach to evaluation and drawing on the views of all those involved.

A14
Ring, 2001[144]

Nature of study
• Action research project to improve the quality of social work practice in a multidisciplinary mental health service, evaluated using a case study design.

Sample and methods
• Mental health division of a local authority housing and SSD providing services to an urban area.
• Baseline assessment of social work practice through self-completion questionnaire to a sample of social workers' clients and audit of 43 case files – used by social workers to develop targets and an action plan.
• Questionnaire survey of 23 social workers and 4 team leaders four months after feedback of baseline assessment: 15 returns.
• Fifteen social workers interviewed after eight months.
• Audit of 44 case files after one year.

What was studied
• Knowledge of findings from baseline assessment, at four and eight months.
• Changes in practice in two priority areas identified and targeted.
• Influences on practice change.
• Views on the importance and feasibility of quality improvements in the priority areas.

Nature of intervention
• Action research.

Quality assessment
- Robust small-scale case study with good details of data collection and analysis

****

B1
Bullock et al, 1998[23]

Nature of study
- Survey of impact of research on social workers' practice.

Sample and methods
- Six local authorities in England and Wales.
- One hundred and sixty-three social workers with direct case responsibility for children and families.
- Age and gender balance broadly reflected national context.
- Questionnaire survey.

What was studied
- What social workers read, to whom they listen, and what difference it makes to their practice.

Quality assessment
- Lacks full information on conduct and content of survey.

B2
Bullock et al, 1998[23]

Nature of study
- Evaluation of use of practice checklists developed from the 'Going Home' research into looked-after children.

Sample and methods
- Nine local authorities in England and Wales, selected to be broadly representative.
- Decision to participate was taken at team level or at directorate level.
- Two of the nine local authorities were involved in experimental studies,

comparing an area where the checklists were used with an area of no intervention.

- Three levels of outcome were assessed:
  - immediate: completion of checklists, assessed through auditing after two years;
  - intermediate: value of intervention for practitioners, assessed using questionnaires and interviews with key individuals after six months;
  - ultimate: changes for service users, assessed through auditing.
- Research team also visited test areas over the initial six-month trial period and gathered data from semi-structured group discussions.

What was studied
- Use of research-based practice checklists following different kinds and intensities of training.

Nature of intervention
- Checklist materials were originally developed through an experimental process involving regular evaluation by different groups.
- Most authorities took checklists blind.
- Social workers underwent varied forms of training in the use of the checklists.
- More intensive training was given in the experimental areas:
  - authority 1: monthly meetings with a professor with research and training experience;
  - authority 2: study day around research materials.

Quality assessment
- Cross-contamination of experimental areas and problems isolating the effects of the intervention. Sometimes difficult to distinguish findings from different sources. Well-considered measures of research use were used.

B3
Tozer and Ray, 1999[172]

Nature of study
- Survey of SSDs' research programmes and of use of research by team managers.

Sample and methods
- Twenty-four SSDs in England, members of RiP.
- Questionnaire to RiP link officers to survey the organisation of the SSDs' research function: 23 responses (96%).
- Questionnaire to family and team managers within the SSDs: 303 responses (43%).

What was studied
- Nature of SSD research programmes, research staff and research dissemination.
- Use of research by team managers, barriers and enablers to this use, and team managers' research needs.

Quality assessment
- Few details about conduct of the survey. Analysis of apparently qualitative and quantitative data unclear. Detailed presentation of original data.

B4
O'Brien and Wrigton, 2001[121]

Nature of study
- Consultation exercise by the Hadley Centre on the use of research in planning for looked-after children.

Sample and methods
- Eight local authorities in South West England.
- Semi-structured interviews with 12 social work childcare and family placement teams in a balance of rural and urban areas:
  - 10 local authority teams;
  - one voluntary agency placement team;
  - one independent foster care agency.
- Telephone interviews with four childcare trainers and six Hadley Centre advisors.

What was studied
- How research is used in permanency planning for children.
- Attitudes to integrating research and practice.

- What resources might support research use.
- What questions research could usefully answer.

Quality assessment
- Appears well conducted but lacks full details on methods of data collection and analysis. No original data are presented to support findings.

B5
Sinclair and Jacobs, 1994[158]

Nature of the study
- National Children's Bureau report of a case study of the use of research in three local authority SSDs, commissioned by the Department of Health.

Sample and methods
- Three local authority sites, providing rural/urban mix.
- Semi-structured interviews with 28 senior personnel.
- Questionnaires surveying team leaders about key pieces of research: 211 responses.

What was studied
- Importance and value placed on research.
- Access to and use of research.
- Barriers and enablers to research use.
- Knowledge, understanding and use of specific pieces of research.

Quality assessment
- Main findings limited to senior personnel but well grounded in original data. Some problematic measures of research 'use'.

B6

Smith, 1995[160]

[Also reported in Smith and Fuller, 1995[161]]

Nature of study

• Pilot project of social workers' research needs and use conducted by the Social Work Research Centre at Stirling University.

Sample and methods

• UK social work practitioners in a range of settings and specialisms, with a bias towards Scotland.
• Postal questionnaire sent to 1,100 practitioners identified through professional organisations: 243 responses.
• Twenty follow-up telephone interviews.

What was studied

• Current practice issues.
• How research is used.
• How research dissemination and links between researchers and practitioners might be improved.

Quality assessment

• Methods clear but difficult to distinguish findings from different sources. Little presentation of original data. Sampling strategy uncertain.

B7

Spittlehouse et al, 2000[164]

Nature of study

• Evaluation of critical appraisal skills workshops for SSDs within CEBSS.

Sample and methods

• Nine SSDs.
• One hundred and eighty-two participants.
• Pre- and post-workshop questionnaires evaluating self-reported knowledge of terms: 134 responses.
• Satisfaction questionnaire: 172 responses.

What was studied
- Change in self-reported understanding of key terms.
- Usefulness and enjoyability of workshops.

Nature of intervention
- CASP workshop adapted for social services after piloting:
  - interactive introductory session giving information on research methods;
  - small group work appraising a RCT;
  - feedback to discuss findings.

Quality assessment
- Aims of study unclear. Evaluation limited in scope but some strong presentation of data. Lacks full details of methods.

B8
Office for Public Management (OPM), 2000[125]

Nature of study
- Review of existing research on the effectiveness of different mechanisms for spreading best practice.

Sample and methods
- Searches of Internet, library and recommended literature.
- Contact with key individuals and relevant organisations.
- Main sources of information were research units, public sector networks, government departments and related agencies, recommended specialists and OPM colleagues.
- Nature of included studies unclear.

What was studied
- Strengths and weaknesses of different dissemination techniques.
- What makes people access and use different types of information.
- The effectiveness of techniques to stimulate innovation.
- Variations across different sectors.

Nature of intervention
- Wide range of different interventions were reviewed.

- Mainly covers:
  - networks;
  - beacons;
  - guidance information;
  - databases;
  - local champions.

Quality assessment
- No systematic search strategy, selection of papers or quality assessment of studies, but covers wide range of literature sources. Origin of findings not always clear.

B9
Hughes et al, 2000[70]

Nature of study
- Review of health and social care literature on disseminating research.

Sample and methods
- Broad search strategy: no details given.
- Studies drawn on include overviews, systematic reviews, discussion papers and case studies.

What was studied
- The range of approaches used to disseminate research in health and social care.
- Evidence of the effectiveness of these approaches and their applicability to social care.
- Examples of change in policy and practice based on research.

Nature of intervention
- Diverse interventions studied within the health care literature.

Quality assessment
- Methods for searching and sifting literature unclear. No quality assessment of included studies.

B10
Hughes et al, 2000[70]

Nature of study
- Review of research dissemination in social care and beyond.

Sample and methods
- Postal questionnaire to 80 diverse research-generating organisations plus telephone follow-up, included higher education institutes, social care agencies, government departments: 57 returns.
- Five focus groups with 52 research users across the UK: included statutory and voluntary sector managers, practitioners and trainers, social work students and educators.
- Twenty-eight individual interviews with key senior personnel within social care and beyond.

What was studied
- Existing initiatives to disseminate research in social care.
- The effectiveness of different approaches to research dissemination.
- What strategies are effective in different contexts.
- Transferable lessons from other fields.

Quality assessment
- Clear aims and wide-ranging study. Sampling strategy uncertain. Sometimes difficult to distinguish findings from different sources.

B11
Fisher, 1997[44]

Nature of study
- Pilot study of social workers' sources and use of knowledge in child protection decisions.

Sample and methods
- Twelve front-line child protection social workers from two SSDs.
- One-to-one interviews.

What was studied
- Quantity and type of training relevant to child protection work.
- Written information available and reading behaviour.
- Experience of supervision and team attitudes to research and theory.

Quality assessment
- Lacks full details of conduct and analysis of study. Limited but carefully examined findings.

B12
Parker et al, 1998[128]

Nature of study
- The EQUAL action research project funded by the European Commission to train volunteers to run reminiscence groups with people with Alzheimer's disease.

Sample and methods
- Sites in Hull (UK), Marseille (France) and Vaxjo (Sweden).
- Aimed to focus on volunteers under 25 and unemployed people but also included students, older unemployed people and people who had retired.
- Recording forms completed by volunteers, individually or as a group.
- Semi-structured interviews with volunteers, staff and sometimes service users.

What was studied
- Extent to which project improved quality of life for participants.
- Volunteer skills development.
- Sustainability of the project.

Nature of intervention
- Action research.

Quality assessment
- Apparently rigorous but reporting of both methods and findings is very condensed. Results presented in summary form with no indication of source.

B13

Atwal, 2002[8]

Nature of study

- Action research study to implement a new interprofessional discharge model for fracture patients in one hospital.

Sample and methods

- Inner–London teaching hospital acute orthopaedic ward.
- Interviews with stakeholders: four nurses, one occupational therapist and one care manager.
- Analysis of integrated care pathways.

What was studied

- Variations from care pathway.
- Stakeholders' views on the discharge model and its impact.

Nature of intervention

- Action research.

Quality assessment

- Clear aims and some presentation of original data. Limited details of methods.

B14

Molas–Gallart et al, 2000[105]

Nature of study

- Examines the impact of the ESRC's AIDS Research Programme.

Sample and methods

- Five-year AIDS Research Programme, 15 projects.
- Forty-three interviews with researchers substantially involved in projects and their dissemination.
- Also interviewed relevant non–academic research users.
- Mapped networks of researchers and users through a snowballing technique.

- Traced post-research activity of researchers such as changes in employment and consultancy roles.

What was studied
- Types of research output.
- Research diffusion channels.
- Forms of research programme impact.

Quality assessment
- Strong underpinning methodology but few details of methods of data collection themselves.

****

C1
Davies, 1994[37]

Nature of study
- Department of Health research review on research impact in the Personal Social Services.

Sample and methods
- Three commissioned reports (one is **B4**): survey, case studies and review of good dissemination initiatives.
- Written documentation from researchers, practitioners, social work educators, voluntary organisations, local and government departments, funding organisations, social work journals.
- Interviews with senior officials in government, research units and other key organisations.

What was studied
- Impact of research on policy and practice.
- Supply, support, mechanisms and infrastructure for research and development.
- Potential role of social work education and training in increasing research impact.

Quality assessment
- No details of methods of commissioned studies that provided some of evidence reported. No details of methods for conducting interviews and collecting written documentation or of sampling strategy.

C2
McCrystal, 2000[99]

Nature of study
- Survey of social workers to assess their views on the Practitioner Research Training Programme at the Queen's University, Belfast.

Sample and methods
- One hundred and forty-four social workers: cross-section of basic grade and middle management.
- Twenty social work teams across 4 Health and Social Services Trusts in Northern Ireland.
- Post-qualifying course at the Queen's University, Belfast.
- Questionnaire administered at team meetings.

What was studied
- Social workers' opinions of and attitudes towards the Practitioner Research Training Programme at the ICCR at Queen's University, Belfast (programme was still under development).
- Also reports on social workers' attitudes to the use of research in practice and how this might be facilitated.

Quality assessment
- Study aims not clearly reflected in findings reported. Lacks full details of methods.

C3
Humphreys and Metcalfe, 2000[72]

Nature of study
- Action research project on recruiting new foster carers.

Sample and methods
- Foster care services in one local authority.
- Dynamic action research process involving data from a variety of sources, including interviews with foster carers.

What was studied
- The effects of including existing foster carers in the recruitment process for new foster carers.

Nature of intervention
- Action research.

Quality assessment
- Sources of data for evaluation of impact of action research unclear. Largely descriptive/anecdotal account.

C4
Cleaver et al, 1998[30]

Nature of study
- Research and development project to identify an effective way of feeding findings from Department of Health research on child protection into practice.

Sample and methods
- Four local authorities in broadly matched pairs.
- Twenty-four initial interviews with front-line social workers and managers to help develop practice tools.
- Questionnaires and meetings with managers assessed field trials of intervention tools.
- Consultations with a range of experienced staff in four original authorities and two further, one voluntary organisation, an advisory group, social work educators and researchers.

What was studied
- How messages from the research might best be disseminated.
- Field trials of prototype intervention tool sover two-month period.
- Assessment of revised intervention tools.

Nature of intervention
- Evidence-based risk assessment tool for the child protection process.
- Prototype tools comprised referral chart and loose leaf data book.
- Revised tools comprised revised referral chart, acting as a reminder rather than a checklist; and a booklet clarifying central research messages into a list of ten 'pitfalls', providing reference to relevant research and acting as an aide memoire.

Quality assessment
- Lack of details about methods and analysis of data related to assessing the value and effectiveness of the tools, rather than their development.

C5
Pahl, 1992[127]

Nature of study
- Assessment of the impact of a piece of locally conducted research on day services for older people.

Sample and methods
- Request sent to those with responsibility for implementing findings for information about action taken.
- Study and implementation took place in local health district area in collaboration with multiagency elderly health care planning team.
- No further details of sample or methods.

Nature of interventions
- Written findings from original research.

What was studied
- Changes in services resulting from recommendations made by a local study on day services for older people.

Quality assessment
- Very briefly described study. Lacks details of methods.

C6
Richardson et al, 1990[140]

Nature of study
- Exercise undertaken on behalf of the (then) DHSS to examine the use and dissemination of research, primarily that commissioned by government.

Sample and methods
- Six general policy areas formed focus of study (acute services, primary health care, nursing, learning disabilities, child care and social security).
- One-to-one and group interviews with:
  - 18 research customers and 44 researchers;
  - 32 individuals in SSDs and 12 in health authorities responsible for policy and practice in two of the six policy areas;
  - 19 individuals responsible for research management within government, research councils and trusts.
- 'Desk research'.
- Exploring ideas at seminars.

What was studied
- Means of improving the use and dissemination of research.
- Means of assessing the use and dissemination of research.

Quality assessment
- Sampling and methods not apparently undertaken in systematic way. No details of analysis of data. Difficult to distinguish findings from authors' own ideas or from wider recommendations.

C7
Tang and Sinclair, 2001[168]

Nature of study
- Examination of the ways in which UK social science researchers exploit the results of their work.

Sample and methods

- Interviews with representative group of 21 university deans, directors, professors, researchers and administrators.
- Case studies of three university projects: units chosen to cover range of methods of dissemination and types of staff.
- Workshop involving 10 external users of social science results and 10 university staff, held towards the end of the project.
- Data are drawn from one of a series of pilot audits.

What was studied

- Nature of exploitation of social science research.
- Attitudes to the exploitation of social science research.
- Constraints on the exploitation of social science research.

Quality assessment

- Few original data are presented and origins of findings are sometimes unclear. Lack of details of methods.

C8
Lyons, 2000[93]

Nature of study

- Paper draws on findings from two previous studies to examine the place of research in social work education.

Sample and methods

- Questionnaires sent to social work departments/units about the Diploma in Social Work content (1994 study).
- Interviews with 11 senior social work academics (1996 study).
- No further details of sample or methods.

What was studied

- Views on teaching social work students about research.
- The extent to which teaching is 'research informed'.

Quality assessment

- Lack of details about aims, methods or analysis of studies for which data are reported. Not always clear that data were originally collected to answer the questions posed of them.

C9

Edwards, 2000[40]

Nature of study

- Case study of research practice collaboration with early years workers including action research to meet the educational demands of the *Desirable Outcomes* initiative.

Sample and methods

- 25 early years workers, diverse backgrounds.
- Nursery setting.
- Research team held monthly workshops with early years workers.
- Data used are self-reflections by participants and field notes.

What was studied

- Early years workers undertaking action research, research-based practice and research-based curriculum development work.

Nature of intervention

- Action research.

Quality assessment

- Lack of details on how data were gathered. Findings appear to draw on other sources of data. Findings not reported for study as a whole.

APPENDIX 6

Database search strategy

All databases were searched as keywords, and from 1980, unless otherwise stated.

FirstSearch – Article First/ECO/ERIC
1990-2003
Searched 24/03/03

#1 (evidence w based) (social w care)
#2 evidence w based & social w care
#3 best-evidence (social w care)
#4 best w evidence (social w care)
#5 (best w evidence w based) (social w care)
#6 evidence-based w practi?e+ (social w care)
#7 evidence-based w polic* (social w care)
#8 research-based w practi?e+ (social w care)
#9 research-based w polic* (social w care)
#10 research w based w change+ (social w care)
#12 evidence w based w change+ (social w care)
#13 research n2 (use or utili*) (social w care)
#14 evidence n2 (use or utili*) (social w care)
#15 research w into w practi?e
#16 evidence w into w practi?e
#17 best w practi?e+ (social w care)
#18 knowledge w based w change
#19 model+ w of w learning & care
#20 model+ w of learning & social w care
#21 model+ n2 learning & social w care
#22 model+ w of w research w utili*
#23 quality w improvement+ & social w care
#24 quality w management & social w care
#25 quality w assurance & social w care
#26 knowledge w (management OR system+)
#27 outcome n research & (social care OR care)

#28 research n2 impediment*

#29 translat* w2 (research OR evidence)

#30 translat* w2 research & social

#31 translat* w2 finding+ & social

#32 translat* w2 result+ &social

#33 effective w practi?e+ & social

#34 connect* n2 research w practi?e

#35 adopt* n2 research & social

#36 adopt* n2 (practi?e OR polic*) & social

#37 adopt* n2 evidence

#38 research n2 access* & social

#39 practi?e-focused

#40 research-focused & social

#41 targetted w dissemination

#42 targetted w diffusion

#43 dissemin* n2 research & social

#44 dissemin* n2 evidence & social

#45 diffusion n2 research & social

#46 diffusion n2 evidence

#47 (research w policy) n2 interaction

#48 (research w practi?e) n2 interaction

#49appli* n2 research & (social OR social w care)

#50 appli* n2 evidence & (social OR social w care)

#51 evidence-led w practi?e+

#52 evidence-based w education w program*

#53 evidence-based & education w program*

#54 learning n2 culture+ & social

#55 learning w culture+ & social

#56 human w resource w management & social

#57 human w resource w management & promotion w2 learning

#58 model+ n2 management & social

#59 model+ n2 human w resource w management

#60 social w care w workforce

#61 research w knowledge w base+

#62 work-based w education

#63 research w minded*

#64 workforce w performance

#65 practi?e w learning

#66 management n2 develop* & social w care

#67 teaching w and w learning

#68 social w work w education

#69 (social w work w education) n2 research

#70 post-qualif* w research

#71 post-qualif* w training

#72 post-qualif* w development

#73 knowledge n2 transform*

#74 social w work & degree w program*

#75 promot* n2 evidence w based w practi?e+

#76 research w based w material+

#77 knowledge n2 source+ & social

#78 theory n1 practi?e w gap

#79 information n1 disseminat* & social

#80 information n1 diffusion & social

#81 learning w culture & social

#82 learning n1 culture & social

#83 research w practi?e w communication+

#84 joining w research w1 practi?e+

#85 research w literate w practi?e+

#86 research w practi?e w dialogue

#87 contribut* n2 (research w1 practi?e+)

#88 research w based w information

#89 effective w practi?e+ & social w care

#90 research w initiative+ & social

#91 what w works & social

#92 barrier+ n1 (research w utili*)

#93 obstacle+ n1 (research w utili*)

#94 barrier+ n1 (research w implement*)

#95 obstacle+ n1 9 research w implement*)

#96 obstacle+ n1 (research w appl*)

#97 barrier+ n1 (research appl*)

#98 (youth w work*) OR (community w work*)

#99 #98 AND (research)

#100 #99 AND (utili* OR use OR appl* OR implement*)

#101 nursery w nurs*

PapersFirst/Proceedings/Geobase

1990-2003

24/03/03

#1 evidence w based & (social w care)

#2 evidence-based & (social w care)

#3 best-evidence

#4 best w evidence

#5 best w evidence w based

#6 evidence w based w practi?e

#7 research w based w practi?e

#8 research w based w change

#9 evidence w based w change

#10 research n2 (use or utili*)

#11 evidence n2 (use or utili*)

#12 research w into w practi?e

#13 evidence w into w practi?e

#15 best w practi?e & (social w care)

#16 knowledge w based w change

#17 model+ w of w learning

#18 model+ n2 learning

#20 model+ w rsearch w utili*

#21 quality w improvement

#22 quality w management

#23 quality w assurance

#24 knowledge w (management OR system)

#25 outcome+ n research & (social w care OR social)

#26 research w impediment

#27 translat* w2 (research OR evidence)

#28 translat* w2 finding+

#29 translat* w2 result+

#30 effective w practi?e+ & (social w care)

#31 connect* n2 research w2 practi?e

#32 adopt* n2 (practi?e OR polic*)

#33 adopt* n2 research

#34 adopt* n2 evidence

#35 research n2 access*

#36 practi?e-focused

#36 research-focused

#37 research –focuse & social

#38 targeted w dissemination

#39 targeted w diffusion

#40 dissemin* n2 research & social

#41 dissemin* n2 evidence

#42 research w policy w interaction

#43 research w practi?e w interaction

#44 appl* n2 research

#45 appl* n2 evidence

#46 evidence-led w practi?e

#47 evidence-based w education w program*

#48 learning n2 culture

#49 learning n2 cultre & social

#50 learning w culture

#51 human w resource w management & social

#52 model+ w of w management

#53 research w knowledge w base

#54 work w based w education

#55 research w minded*

#56 workforce w performance

#57 practi?e w learning

#58 teaching w and w learning

#59 post w qualif* w research

#60 knowledge w transfer & social

#61 knowledge n1 transfer & social

#62 research w based w material+

#63 knowledge w source+

#64 theory w practi?e gap

#65 information n2 dissemination & social

#66 information n2 diffusion & social

#67 learning w culture

#68 research w based w information

#69 what w works & social

#70 barrier+ w to w research

#71 obstacle+ w to w research

#72 youth w work* OR community w work*

#73 #72 AND research w utili*

#74 #72 AND research

#75 #72 AND research (utili* OR use OR appl* OR implement*)

#76 nursery w nurs*

#77#76 AND research (utili* OR use OR appl* OR implement*)

****

Web of Science
28/03/03

#1 evidence base social care

#2 evidence based social

#3 evidence based SAME social

#4 best evidence based social

#5 best evidence based SAME social

#6 evidence based practi* AND (social care OR social work)

#7 evidence based practi* SAME social

#8 research based practi* AND (social care OR social work)

#9 research based practi* SAME social

#10 research based change

#11 evidence based change

#12 (research OR evidence) SAME (use OR utili*)

#13 (research OR evidence) SAME & (social care OR social work)

#14 research into practi* & (social care OR social work)

#15 evidence into practi* & (social care OR social work)

#16 best practi* & (social care OR social work)

#17 evaluation (use OR utili*) & (social care OR social work)

#18 effective practi* & (social care OR social work)

#19 knowledge based change*

#20 what works & (social care OR social work)

#21 (implement* OR use OR appl* OR utili*) SAME (research or evidence) AND (social care OR social work)

#22 dissemination SAME (research OR evidence) & (social care OR social work)

#23 diffusion SAME (research OR evidence)

#24 research SAME (diffusion OR dissemination)

#25 (barriers OR obstacles) to research

#26 (barriers OR obstacles) to research AND (implement* OR use OR appl* OR utili*)

#27 models of learning

#28 models SAME learning AND (social care OR social work)

#29 models SAME research utili*

#30 continu* SAME (education OR professional development) & (social care OR social work)

#31 practi* guide* AND (social care OR social work)

#32 information management & (social care OR social work)

#33 information management system & (social care OR social work)

#34 quality management & (social care OR social work)

#35 outcome research & (social care OR social work)

#36 research outcome

#37 translat* SAME (research OR findings OR results)

#38 research initiative* & (social care OR social work)

#39 adopt* SAME (research OR evidence) & (social care OR social work)

#40 (connecting research and practice*)

#41 research SAME constraint* & (social care OR social work)

#42 practi#e focus*

#43 research focus* & (social care OR social work)

#44 targeted dissemination OR targeted diffusion

#45 rsearch practi#e interaction

#46 research led practi#e

#47 research transfer

#48 research SAME transfer

#49 research communication

#50 research SAME communication

#51 implementation stateg*

#52 implementation SAME strateg*

#53 evidence-focused

#54 evidence led practi#e

#55 contribut* SAME research to practi#e

#56 research literate practi#e

#57 dissemination strateg*

#58 research based information

#59 research minded*

#60 empirical SAME (research OR findings OR evidence) & (social care OR social work)

#61 adopt* of research

#62 research application

#63 research SAME application & (social care OR social work)

#64 knowledge transformation

#65 research practi#e dialogue

#66 human resource management

#67 human resource management SAME polic★

#68 human resource management SAME polic★ & (social care OR social work)

#69 evidence based teaching

#70 evidence based learning

#71 post-qualifying research

#72 promot★ SAME evidence based practi#e

#73 promo★ evidence based practi#e

#74 user care involvement

#75 research based materials

#76 research knowledge base

#77 social care workforce AND research utili★

#78 social work workforce AND research utili★

#79 models of management AND (social care OR social work)

#80 social care management

#81 social work management

#82 learning culture

#83 evidence based education★ program★

#84 theory practi#e gap

#85 practi#e theory gap

#86 professional learning

#87 professional learning & (social work OR social care)

#88 youth work

#89 youth work & research

#90 community work★

#91 community work★ AND research

★★★

CareData

31/03/03

#1 evidence based practice

#2 dissemination of research

#3 action research & social work★/social care★

#4 applied research & social work★/social care★

#5 access to information & social work★/social care★

#6 social work education & evidence★

#7 accreditation

#8 accreditation & social work courses

#9 accreditation & practice placement

#10 accreditation & practice teachers/teaching

#11 further education & social work/social care

#12 best value

#13 best value & social work

#14 quality assurance & social work*/social care*

#15 quality assurance & evidence*

#16 standards & social work

#17 social work education w6 standards

#18 innovation in practice

#19 innovation* & research*

#20 change p2 management

#21 change w2 management

#22 quality assurance

#23 criminal justice & social work* & research

#24 evidence* & criminal justice

#25 evidence based* & criminal justice OR crime

#26 decision making and research*

#27 decision making and social work*/social care*

#28 diploma in social work and research*

#29 diploma in social work and evidence*

#30 national vocational qualification and research*

#31 national vocational qualification and evidence*

#32 qualifications and research*

#33 qualifications and evidence*

#34 post qualifying education

#35 post qualifying education and evidence*

#36 post qualifying education and research*

#37 social work education

#38 social work education and evidence*

#39 social work education and research*

#40 staff development

#41 staff development and evidence*

#42 staff development and research*

#43 student social workers

#44 student social workers and evidence*

#45 student social workers and research*

#46 management and social work*/social care*

#47 management

#48 research methods

#49 teaching methods

#50 teaching methods and research★

#51 teaching methods and evidence★

#52 employment p2 research

#53 evaluation p2 research

#54 social work methods

#55 social work methods and evidence★

#56 performance evaluation

#57 hospital social work★

#58 medical social work★

#59 information and communication technology

#60 information and communication technology and social work★

#61 information and communication technology and social care

#62 information services and social work★/social care

#63 management information systems

#64 information management and social care★/social work★

#65 information and change

#66 innovation p2 change

#67 social services departments and research★

#68 keyworkers

#69 knowledge management

#70 knowledge management and social work★/social care★

#71 literature reviews

#72 personnel management and research★

#73 objective setting and management

#74 innovation and management

#75 managers and research★

#76 managers and evidence based practice

#77 managers and evidence★

#78 models and learning

#79 models and manage★

#80 organisational structures and research★

#81 community social work

#82 community social work and research★

#83 performance monitoring and research★

#84 applied research and social workers★

#85 psychiatric social work and research

#86 psychiatric social work and evidence★

#87 qualifications and social work★ and research

#88 social work contracts and research

#89 social worker user relationship and research

#90 teaching methods

#91 teaching methods and research★

#92 teaching methods and evidence★

#93 youth work

#94 youth work and research

#95 community work

#96 community work and research

#97 nursery nurs★

****

CSA ASSIA/BHI/PAIS/Sociological Abstracts/Social Services Abstracts

1990>

07/04/03

#1 evidence-based

#2 evidence-based practi?e

#3 best evidence based

#4 research based practi?e

#5 (research|evidence) based change

#6 (research|evidence) (use|utili★)

#7 evidence utili/ation

#8 (research|evidence) into practi?e

#9 best practi?e

#10 identif★ best practi?e

#11 dissemin★ best practi?e

#12 best practi?e AND (teaching "and" learning)

#13 evidence-based practi?e AND social (care★|work★)

#14 evidence-based AND social (care★|work★)

#15 research utili?ation AND social (care★|work★)

#16 what works

#17 what works AND social (care★|work★)

#18 knowledge based change

#19 model★ of learning AND social (care★|work★)

#20 model★ of research utili★

#21 quality improvement*

#22 quality management

#23 quality assurance

#24 outcome research

#25 (research) within3 (impediment)

#26 translat* within3 (research|evidence)

#27 translat* within3 finding*

#28 translat* within3 result*

#29 effective practi?e*

#30 connecting (research and practi?e)

#31 adopt* research

#32 adopt* of research

#33 adopt* evidence

#34 practi?e focused

#35 research focused

#36 targeted (dissemination|diffusion)

#37 (evidence|research) w3 (disemination|diffusion)

#38 research practi?e interaction

#39 (appli*|utili*|use|implement*) (research|evidence)

#40 (evidence|research) led

#41 evidence-based education

#42 learning culture

#43 models of management

#44 research minded*

#45 (barrier*|obstacle*) AND research

#46 (barrier*|obstacle*) to research (appl*|use|utili*|implement*)

#47 human resource management AND social (care*|work*)

#48 criminal justice AND social (care*|work*)

#49 continuing professional development

#50 post qualifying education

#51 workplace education

#52 (decision making) within4 (research)

#53 social (work|care) education AND (research|evidence)

#54 organi?ational culture AND social (care*|work*)

#55 workplace learning

#56 (community|health|medical|hospital|psychiatic) social (care*|work*)

#57 (innovation) w3 (change)

#58 diffusion of innovation

#59 personnel management

#60 (management | manager★) AND evidence-based

#61 teaching method★ AND social (care★ | work★)

#62 empirical research AND social (care★ | work★)

#63 commissioned research AND (appl★ | use | utili★ | implement★)

#64 constraint★ AND research (appl★ | use | utili★ | implement★)

#65 research within2 accessibl★

#66 constraint★ within3 research (appl★ | use | utili★ | implement★)

#67 research within2 assimil★

#68 research AND implementation strateg★

#69 strategic (appl★ | use | utili★ | implement★) AND (research | evidence)

#70 knowledge trans★

#71 research model★

#72 research model★ AND social (care★ | work★)

#73 community care AND (research | evidence)

#74 community care AND research (appl★ | use | utili★ | implement★)

#75 practi?e-research

#76 linking research within2 practi?e

★★★

Community Care (www.community-care.co.uk)
Article search 1995>
28/04/03

#1 evidence based practice

#2 best evidence based

#3 research based practice

#4 evidence based policy

#5 research based policy

#6 best practice

#7 research into practice

#8 evidence into practice

#9 research utilisation

#10 what works

#11 research implementation

#12 implementation guidelines

#13 barriers to research

#14 information management

#15 models of learning

#16 quality improvement

#17 quality assurance

#18 connecting research and practice

#19 practice-focused

#20 research application

#21 research transfer

#22 evidence-led

#23 diffusion of innovations

#24 dissemination of research

#25 social care education

#26 evidence based teaching

#27 post qualifying research

#28 knowledge utilisation

#29 social care management

#30 evidence based education

#31 research-practice gap

#32 youth work★

#33 youth work★ and research utili★

#34 youth work★ and research appl★

#35 youth work★ and research implementation

#36 youth work★ and research use

#37 community work★

#38 community work★ and research utili★

#39 community work★ and research appl★

#40 community work★ and research implementation

#41 community work★ and research use

#42 nursery nurs★

#43 nursery nurs★ and research

#44 nursery nurs★ and research use

#45 nursery nurs★ and research implementation

#46 nursery nurse and research appl★

#47 nursery nurse and research utili★

OVID- SIGLE
1985-2002
09/05/03

#1 evidence based
#2 evidence based practi?e
#3 best evidence based
#4 research based practi?e
#5 (research OR evidence) based change
#6 (research OR evidence) utili*
#7 evidence utili*
#8 (research OR evidence) into practi?e
#9 best pract?e
#10 identif* best practi?e
#11 disseminat* best practi?e
#12 best practi?e AND (teaching and learning)
#13 evidence based practi?e AND (social (care* OR work*))
#14 evidence based AND (social (care OR work*))
#15 research utili?ation
#16 what works
#17 what works AND (social (care* OR work*))
#18 knowledge based change
#19 model* of research utili*
#20 model* of learning AND (social (care* OR work*)
#21 quality improvement*
#22 quality management
#23 quality assurance AND (social (care* OR work*))
#24 outcome research
#25 research impediment*
#26 translat* research
#27 translat* finding*
#28 translat* result*
#29 effective practi?e*
#30 connect* (research AND practi?e)
#31 adopt* research
#32 adopt* of research
#33 adopt* evidence
#34 practi?e focus*
#35 research focus*

#36 targeted dissemination

#37 targeted diffusion

#38 diffusion AND evidence

#39 research practi?e interaction

#40 appl* of (research OR evidence)

#41 implement* of (research OR evidence)

#42 use of (research OR evidence)

#43 (evidence OR research) led

#44 evidence based education

#45 learning culture*

#46 models of management

#47 research minded*

#48(barrier* OR obstacle*) to (research OR change)

#49 human resource management

#50 criminal justice AND (social (care* OR work*))

#51 continuing professional development

#52 post qualifying education

#53 workplace education

#54 (decision making) AND research

#55 (social (work* OR care*) education)

#56 organi?ational culture*

#57 workplace learning

#58 (innovation and change)

#59 diffusion of innovation

#60 personnel management

#61 management AND evidence based

#62 teaching method* AND (social (care* OR work*))

#63 empirical research AND (social (care* OR work*))

#64 commissioned research AND (use OR utili* OR appl* OR implement*)

#65 constraint* AND research

#66 research accessib*

#67 research assimilation

#68 research AND implementation strateg*

#69 knowledge transformation

#70 learning based change

#71 social work* AND (diploma OR NVQ OR national vocational qualification OR degree)

#72 post qualifying research

#73 learning disabl*

#74 learning disabl★ AND (research OR evidence OR practi?e)

#75 learning disabl★ AND (use OR utili★ OR appl★ OR implement★)

#76 #74 AND #75

#77 (abuse OR neglect) and (use OR utili★ OR appl★ OR implement★)

#78 (abuse OR neglect) and (research OR evidence)

#79 (abuse OR neglect) and (social (work★ OR care★))

#80 #77 AND #78

#81 (elder★ OR child★ OR adolescen★) AND (use OR utili★ OR appl★ OR implement★)

#82 (elder★ OR child★ OR adolescen★) AND (research OR evidence OR practi?e)

#83 (elder★ OR child★ OR adolescen★) AND (social (work★ OR care★))

#84 #81 AND #82

#83 (young people OR older people OR geriatric) AND (use OR utili★ OR appl★ OR implement★)

#84 (young people OR older people OR geriatric) AND (research OR evidence OR practi?e)

#85 (young people OR older people OR geriatric) AND (social (work★ OR care★))

#86 #83 AND #84

#87 homeless★ AND (social care★ OR social work★)

#88 homeless★ AND (research OR evidence OR practi?e)

#89 homeless★ AND (use OR utili★ OR appl★ OR implement★)

#90 #88 AND #89

#91 (mental ill★ OR mental health) AND (use OR utili★ OR appl★ OR implement★)

#92 (mental ill★ OR mental health) AND (research OR evidence OR practi?e)

#93 (mental ill★ OR mental health) AND (social care★ OR social work★)

#94 #91 AND #92

#95 (substance use OR substance misuse) AND (use OR utili★ OR appl★ OR implement★)

#96 (substance use OR substance misuse) AND (research OR evidence OR practi?e)

#97 (substance use OR substance misuse) AND (social care★ OR social work★)

#98 #95 AND #96

#99 alcohol★ AND (use OR utili★ OR appl★ OR implement★)

#100 alcohol★ AND (research OR evidence OR practi?e)

#101 alcohol★ AND (social care★ OR social work★)

#102 #99 AND #100

#103 (child protection) AND (social (care★ OR work★))

#104 (child protection) AND (research OR evidence OR practi?e)

#105 (child protection) AND (use OR utili★ OR appl★ OR implement★)

#106 #104 AND#105

#107 (respite OR foster OR domicil★ OR residential OR day OR community) AND (social (care★ OR work★))

#108 (respite OR foster OR domicil★ OR residential OR day OR community) AND (research OR evidence OR practi?e)

#109 (respite OR foster OR domicil★ OR residential OR day OR community) AND (use OR utili★ OR appl★ OR implement★)

#110 #108 AND #109

#111 (early years OR early intervention) AND (research OR evidence OR practi?e)

#112 (early years OR early intervention) AND (social (care★ OR work★))

****

FirstSearch – Medline

1990-2003

16/05/03

#1 evidence w based

#2 evidence w based w practi?e

#3 best w evidence w based

#4 research w based w practi?e

#5 (research OR evidence) w based w change

#6 (research OR evidence) w utili?ation

#7 (research OR evidence) into w practi?e

#8 (best practi?e) AND (social (care★ OR work★))

#9 identif★ w1 best w practi?e

#10 dissemin★ w1 best w practi?e

#11 best w practi?e AND (teaching and learning)

#12 evidence w based w practi?e AND (social (care★ OR work★))

#13 evidence w based AND (social (care★ OR work★))

#14 research w utili★

#15 what w works

#16 what w works AND (social (care★ OR work★))

#17 knowledge w based w change

#18 models+ of learning AND (social (care★ OR work★))

#19 model+ of research w utili* AND (social (care* OR work*)

#20 quality w management AND (social (care* OR work*)

#21 quality w improvement AND (social (care* OR work*)

#22 quality assurance AND (social (care* OR work*)

#23 outcome w research AND (social (care* OR work*)

#24 research w impediment AND (social (care* OR work*)

#25 translat* w research AND (social (care* OR work*)

#26 translat* w find* AND (social (care* OR work*)

#27 translat* w result* AND (social (care* OR work*)

#28 effective w practi?e+

#29 connect* (research AND practi?e)

#30 adopt* w1 research

#31 adopt* w1 evidence

#33 practi?e w focused

#33 research w focused AND (social (care* OR work*)

#34 targeted w dissemination

#35 targeted w diffusion

#36 diffusion w2 evidence

#37 research w practi?e w interaction

#38 appl* w1 research AND (social (care* OR work*)

#39 appl* w evidence AND (social (care* OR work*)

#40 use w of w research AND (social (care* OR work*)

#41 use w of evidence AND (social (care* OR work*)

#42 (use OR util* OR appl* OR implement*)

#43 #50 AND research

#44 #50 AND evidence

#45 evidence w led

#46 evidence w based w education

#47 learning w culture

#48 models w of w management

#49 research w minded*

#50 barrier* w2 research

#51 obstacle* w2 research

#52 human w resource w management

#53 criminal w justice AND (social w care* OR social w work*)

#54 continuing w professional w development

#55 post w qualifying w education

#56 workplace w education

#57 decision w making AND education AND (social w care* OR social w work*)

#58 ((social w work* OR social w care*) education) AND research

#59 #42 AND #58

#60 organi?ational w culture+ AND (social w care* OR social w work*)

#61 workplace w learning

#62 innovation w1 change

#63 diffusion w of w innovation* AND (social w care* OR social w work*)

#64 personnel w management

#65 management AND evidence w based

#66 teaching w method* AND (social w care* OR social w work*)

#67 constraint* AND research

#68 constraint* n1 research

#69 research n1 accessibl*

#70 research n1 assimilation

#71 research w implementation w strateg*

#72 knowledge n1 transformation

#73 (diploma OR NVQ OR national w vocational w qualification) AND (social w care* OR social w work*)

#74 post w qualifying w research

#75 learning w disabl* AND (research OR evidence OR practi?e)

#76 #75 AND (use OR utili* OR appl* OR implement*)

#77 #76 AND (social w care* OR social w work*)

#78 (abuse OR neglect) AND (research OR evidence OR practi?e)

#79 #78 AND (use OR utili* OR appl* OR implement*)

#80 #79 AND (social w care* OR social w work*)

#81 (elder OR adolscent* OR child*) AND (research OR evidence OR practi?e)

#82 #81 AND (use OR utili* OR appl* OR implement*)

#83 #82 AND (social w care* OR social w work*)

#84 (young w people OR older w people OR geriatric) AND (research OR evidence OR practi?e)

#85 #84 AND (use OR utili* OR appl* OR implement*)

#86 #85 AND (social w care* OR social w work*)

#87 homeless* AND (research OR evidence OR practi?e)

#88 #87 AND (use OR utili* OR appl* OR implement*)

#89 #88 AND (social w care* OR social w work*)

#90 (mental w ill* OR mental w health) AND (research OR evidence OR practi?e)

#91 #90 AND (use OR utili★ OR appl★ OR implement★)

#92 #91AND (social w care★ OR social w work★)

#93 (substance w use OR substance w misuse) AND (social w care OR social w work★)

#94 alcohol★ AND (social w care★ OR social w work★)

#95 #94AND (research OR evidence)

#96 #95 AND (use OR utili★ OR appl★ OR implement★)

#97 (child w protection) AND (social w care★ OR social w work★)

#98 #97 AND (research OR evidence)

#99 #98 AND (use OR utili★ OR appl★ OR implement★)

#100 (respite OR foster OR domicil★ OR day Or community) AND (care OR services)

#101 #100 AND (research OR evidence)

#102 #101 AND (use OR utili★ OR appl★ OR implement★)

#103 (early w years OR early w intervention)

#104 #103 AND (research OR evidence)

#105 #104 AND (social w care★ OR social w work★)

#106 #105 AND (use OR utili★ OR appl★ OR implement★)

#107 (youth w work★) Or (community w work★)

#108 #107 and research w use

#108 #107 and research w utili★

#109 #107 and research w appl★

#110 #107 and research w implement★

#111 nursery w nurs★

#112 #111 and research w use

#113 #111 and research w appl★

#114 #111 and research w mplement★

#115 #111 and research utili★

★★

IBSS- BIDS

19/05/03

#1 evidence based

#2 evidence based practice

#3 best evidence based

#4 research based practice

#5 (evidence OR research) based change

#6 research utili*

#7 evidence utili*

#8 research into practice

#9 evidence into practice

#10 best practice

#11 identif* AND best practice

#12 dissemin* AND best practice

#13 best practice AND (teaching and learning)

#14 evidence based practice AND (social care* OR social work*)

#15 what works

#16 knowledge based change

#17 model* of learning

#18 model* of research util*

#19 quality improvement*

#20 quality management

#21 quality assurance

#22 outcome research

#23 research impediment

#24 translat* research

#25 translt* finding*

#26 translat* result*

#27 effective practice*

#28 connecting AND (research and practice)

#29 adopt* research

#30 adoption of research

#31 adopt* evidence

#32 practice focus*

#33 research focused

#34 targeted dissemination

#35 targeted diffusion

#36 diffusion AND (evidence OR research)

#37 research practice interaction

#38 appl* of (research OR evidence)

#39 implementation of (research OR evidence)

#40 use of (evidence OR research)

#41 evidence led

#42 research led

#43 learning culture*

#44 model* of management

#45 research minded*

#46 barrier* AND (research OR evidence)

#47 human resource management AND social

#48 criminal justice AND (social work* OR social care*)

#49 continuing professional development

#50 post qualifying education

#51 workplace education

#52 (decision making AND research) AND (social care* OR social work*)

#53 social work education

#54 organi* culture*

#55 workplace learning

#56 (innovation AND change) AND (social)

#57 diffusion of innovation*

#58 personnel management AND social

#59 management AND evidence based

#60 teaching method*

#61 constraint* AND (research OR evidence)

#62 (research AND access*) AND social

#63 research accessibility

#64 research assimilation

#65 assimilat* AND research

#66 implementation strateg*

#67 knowledge transf*

#68 learning based change

#69 (diploma OR degree OR NVQ OR national vocational qualification) AND (social work* OR social care*)

#70 post qualifying research

#71 learing disabli* AND (social work* OR social care*)

#72 learning disabl* AND (research OR evidence)

#73 learning disabl* AND (implement* OR use OR appl* OR utili*)

#74 (abuse OR neglect) AND (social care* OR social work*)

#75 (abuse OR neglect) AND (research OR evidence)

#76 (abuse OR neglect) AND (implement* OR use OR appl* OR utili*)

#77 (elder* OR child OR adolescent*) AND (social care* OR social work*)

#78 (elder* OR child OR adolescent*) AND (research OR evidence)

#79 (elder* OR child OR adolescent*) AND (implement* OR use OR appl* OR utili*)

#80 (young people OR old* people OR geriatric) AND (social care* OR social work*)

#81 (young people OR old* people OR geriatric) AND (research OR evidence)

#82 (homeless*) AND (social care* OR social work*)

#83 (mental ill* OR mental health) AND (social care* OR social work*)

#84 #83 AND (research OR evidence)

#85 (substance use OR substance misuse) AND (social care* OR social work*)

#86 (alcohol*) AND (social care* OR social work*)

#87 (child protection) AND (social care* OR social work*)

#88 #87 AND (research OR evidence)

#89 (respite OR foster OR domicil* OR residential OR day OR community) AND (care OR service*)

#90 #89 AND (social care* OR social work*)

#91 #90 AND (research OR evidence)

#92 (early years OR early intervention) AND (social care* OR social work*)

#93 youth work*

#94 community work*

#95 nursery nurs*

****

Expanded Academic ASAP (advanced search)
23/05/03

#1 evidence w based

#2 evidence w based w practi?e

#3 best w evidence w based

#4 research w based w practi?e

(evidence OR research) w based w change

#6 research w utili*

#7 evidence w utili*

#8 research w into w practi?e

#9 evidence w into w practi?e

#10 best w practi?e and (social w care* OR social w work*)

#11 identif* n2 best w practi?e

#12 dissemin* n2 best w practi?e

#13 best w practi?e AND (teaching and learning)

#14 evidence w based AND (social w care* OR social w work*)

#15 what works AND (social w care* OR social w work*)

#16 knowledge w based w change

#17 model* w of w learning

#18 model* n2 research w utili*

#19 quality w improvement*

#20 quality w management AND (social w care* OR social w work*)

#21 quality w assurance AND (social w care* OR social w work*)

#22 outcome w research

#23 research w impediment!

#24 translat* n1 research

#25 translat* n1 finding*

#26 translat* n1 result*

#27 effective w practi?e!

#28 connecting w (research and practi?e)

#29 adopt* w1 research

#30 adopt* w1 evidence

#31 practi?e w focused

#32 research w focused

#33 targeted w dissemination

#34 targeted w diffusion

#35 research w practi?e w interaction

#36 appl* n (research OR evidence) AND (social w care* OR social w work*)

#37 use n (research OR evidence) AND (social w care* OR social w work*)

#38 implement* n (research OR evidence) AND (social w care* OR social w work*)

#39 evidence w led

#40 research w led

#41 learning w culture!

#42 model* n1 management AND (social w care* OR social w work*)

#43 research w minded*

#44 barrier* n1 research

#45 human w resource w management AND (social w care* OR social w work*)

#46 criminal w justice AND (social w care* OR social w work*)

#47 continuing w professional w development

#48 post w qualifying w education

#49 (decision w making AND research) AND (social w care* OR social w work*)

#50 (social w work OR social w care*) w education

#51 organi* w culture

#52 workplace w learning

#53 (innovation! n2 change) AND (social w care* OR social w work*)

#54 diffusion n2 innovation!

#55 personnel w management

#56 management AND evidence w based

#57 teaching w method* AND (social w care* OR social w work*)

#58 constraint* n3 research

#59 research w access*

#60 research n2 access*

#61 research n2 assimi*

#62 implement* n1 strateg*

#63 knowledge n1 transform*

#64 (early w years OR early w intervention) AND (social w care* OR social w work*)

#65 learning w based w change

#66 diploma OR degree OR NVQ OR national w vocational w qualification

#67 #66 AND (social w care* OR social w work*)

#68 post w qualifying w research

#69 (learning disabl* OR disabl*) AND (social w care* OR social w work*)

#70 #69 AND (research OR evidence)

#71 (abuse OR neglect) AND (social w care* OR social w work*)

#72 #71 AND (research OR evidence)

#73 #72 AND (use OR utili* OR appl* OR implement*)

#74 (elder* OR child* OR adolescent*) AND (social w care* OR social w work*)

#75 #74 AND (research OR evidence)

#76 #75 AND (use OR utili* OR appl* OR implement*)

#77 (young w people OR older w people OR geriatric) AND (social w care* OR social w work*)

#78 #77 AND (research OR evidence)

#79 #78 AND (use OR utili* OR appl* OR implement*)

#80 homeless* AND (social w care* OR social w work*)

#81 #80 AND (research OR evidence)

#82 (mental w ill* OR mental w health) AND (social w care* OR social w work*)

#83 #82 AND (research OR evidence)

#84 #83 AND (use OR utili* OR appl* OR implement*)

#85 (substance w use OR substance w misuse) AND (social w care* OR social w work*)

#86 alcohol* AND (social w care* OR social w work*)

#87 #86 AND (research OR evidence)

#88 child w protection AND (social w care* OR social w work*)

#89 (respite Or foster OR domicil* OR residential OR day OR community)
   AND (care* OR service*)

#90 #89 AND (social w care* OR social w work*)

#91 #90 AND (research OR evidence)

#92 #91 AND (use OR utili* OR appl* OR implement*)

#93 community w work*

#94 #93 and research

#95 #93 and research w utili*

#96 #93 and research n utili*

#97 youth w work*

#98 #97 and research

#99 nursery w nurs*

****

Cochrane Database (Systematic Reviews/Abstracts of Reviews of Effects/Register of Controlled Trials)

(Free Text Searching)

29/05/03

#1 evidence-based

#2 evidence-based practice

#3 best evidence based

#4 research based practice

#5 evidence based change

#6 research based change

#7 research utili*

#8 evidence utili*

#9 research into practice

#10 evidence into practice

#11 best practice

#12 identi* best practice

#13 dissemin* best practice

#14 best practice AND (teaching and learning)

#15 evidence based AND (social care* OR social work*)

#16 what works

#17 knowledge based change

#18 model* of learning

#19 model* of research utili*

#20 quality management

#21 quality improvement★ AND (social care★ OR social work★)

#22 quality assurance AND (social care★ OR social work★)

#23 outcome research

#24 research impediment

#25 translat★ NEAR research

#26 translat★ NEAR finding★

#27 translat★ NEAR result★

#28 effective practice★

#29 connect★ NEAR (research and practice)

#30 (adopt★ NEAR research) OR (adopt★ NEAR evidence)

#32 practice focused

#33 research focused

#34 targeted dissemination

#35 targeted diffusion

#36 research practice interaction

#37 appl★ of (research OR evidence)

#38 use of (research OR evidence)

#39 implement★ of (research OR evidence)

#40 evidence led

#41 research led

#42 learning culture

#43 model★ NEAR management

#44 research minded★

#45 barrier★ NEAR research

#46 human resource management

#47 criminal justice and (social care★ OR social work)

#48 continuing professional development

#49 post qualifying education

#50 decision making NEAR research

#51 social work education

#52 organi★ culture★

#53 innovation NEAR change

#54 workplace learning

#55 diffusion NEAR innovation★

#56 personnel management

#57 management AND evidence based

#58 teaching method★

#59 constraint★ NEAR research

#60 research NEAR access*

#61 research access*

#62 research assimil*

#63 implement* strateg*

#64 knowledge NEAR transform*

#65 learning based change

#66 ((diploma OR degree OR NVQ OR national vocational qualification) AND
(social care* OR social work*))

#67 post qualifying research

#68 ((learning disabl* OR disabl*) AND (social work* OR social care*))

#69 ((learning disabl* OR disabl*) AND (research OR evidence))

#70 ((abuse OR neglect) AND (social work* OR social care*))

#71 ((abuse OR neglect) AND (research OR evidence))

#72 ((elder* OR child* OR adolescent*) AND (social work* OR social care*))

#73 ((elder* OR child* OR adolescent*) AND (research OR evidence))

#74 ((elder* OR child* OR adolescent*) AND (utili* OR appl* OR
implement* OR use))

#75 ((young people OR older people OR geriatric) AND (social work* OR
social care*))

#76 ((young people OR older people OR geriatric) AND (research OR
evidence))

#77 ((young people OR older people OR geriatric) AND (utili* OR appl* OR
implement* OR use))

#78 homeless* AND (social work* OR social care*)

#79 ((mental ill* OR mental health) AND (social work* OR social care*))

#80 ((mental ill* OR mental health) AND (research OR evidence))

#81 ((mental ill* OR mental health) AND (utili* OR appl* OR implement*
OR use))

#82 ((substance use OR substance misuse) AND (social work* OR social care*))

#83 alcohol* AND (social work* OR social care*))

#84 alcohol* AND (research OR evidence))

#85 child protection AND (social work* OR social care*))

#86 ((respite OR foster OR domicil* OR community OR day OR residential)
AND (care* OR service*))

#87 #86 AND (social work* OR social care*)

#88 #86 AND (research OR evidence)

#89 #86 AND (utili* OR appl* OR implement* OR use)

#90 ((early years OR early intervention) AND (social work* OR social care*))

#91 community work*

#92 community work* and research
#93 #92 and (utili* Or use OR appl* Or implement*)
#94 youth work*
#95 nursery nurs*

****

BEI Education-line
Index search (any field)/Thesaurus RT/LT etc)
29/05/03

#1 evidence based
#2 evidence base
#3 evidence driven
#4 evidence informed
#5 evidence-aware
#6 evidence-based
#7 evidence-bases
#8 evidence-influenced
#9 evidence-informed
#11 best practice
#13 best-evidence
#14 best-practice
#15 best-evidence based
#16 research aware
#17 research based
#18 research driven
#19 research-practitioners
#20 research grounded
#21 research informed
#22 research led
#23 dissemination
#24 teaching and learning
#25 what works
#26 knowledge based
#27 knowledge centred
#28 knowledge-in-practice
#29 model-based
#30 quality assurance

#31 outcome focused

#32 outcome based

#33 outcome driven

#34 outcome led

#35 utilisation-focused

#36 decision making

#37 social work

#38 disability

#39 disabled

#40 abuse: child

#41 abuse: drug

#42 abuse: elder

#43 abuse: sexual

#44 child welfare

#45 children-at-risk

#46 geriatric

#47 homeless

#48 mental health

#49 foster-

#50 early-

#51 youth worker

#52 youth service

#53 community services

#54 nursery nurses

****

Planex (Guided Search)
02/06/03

#1 evidence based

#2 evidence based practice

#3 best AND evidence based

#4 research utili*

#5 research based policy

#5 research based practice

#6 (research OR evidence) AND based change

#7 evidence utili*

#8 research into practice

#9 evidence into practice

#10 best practice

#11 identif* AND best practice

#12 dissemin* AND best practice

#13 best practice AND (teaching and learning)

#14 evidence based AND (social care* OR social work*)

#15 what works

#16 knowledge based change

#17 model* of learning

#18 model* of research utili*

#19 quality improvement*

#20 quality management AND (social care* OR social work*)

#21 quality assurance AND (social care* OR social work*)

#22 outcome research

#23 research impediment*

#24 translat* AND research

#25 translat* AND result*

#26 translat* AND finding*

#27 (effective AND practice*) AND (social care* OR social work*)

#28 connecting AND (research AND practice)

#29 (adopt* AND (research OR evidence)) AND (social care* OR social work*)

#30 practice focused

#31 research focused

#32 targeted AND dissemination

#33 targeted AND diffusion

#34 research practice interaction

#35 appl* (research OR evidence)

#36 implement* (research OR evidence)

#37 use (research OR evidence)

#38 evidence led

#39 research led

#40 learning culture

#41 models AND management AND (social care* OR social work*)

#42 research minded*

#43 barriers to research

#44 human resource management

#45 criminal justice AND (social care* OR social work*)

#46 continuing professional development AND (social care* OR social work*)

#47 post qualifying education

#48 (decision making AND research) AND (social care* OR social work*)

#49 social work education

#50 organisational culture AND (social care* OR social work*)

#51 workplace learning

#52 innovation AND change AND (social care* OR social work*)

#53 diffusion AND innovation*

#54 personnel management

#55 management AND evidence based

#56 teaching method*

#57 constraint* AND research

#58 (research AND access*) AND (social care* OR social work*)

#59 research AND assimil*

#60 implement* strateg* AND (social care* OR social work*)

#61 knowledge AND transform*

#62 learning based change

#63 (diploma OR degree OR NVQ OR national vocation qualification) AND (social care* OR social work*)

#64 (learning disabl* OR disabl*) AND (social care* OR social work*)

#65 #64 AND (research OR evidence)

#66 #65 AND (use OR implement* OR appl* OR utili*)

#67 (abuse OR neglect) AND (social care* OR social work*)

#68 #67 AND (research OR evidence)

#69 68 AND (use OR implement* OR appl* OR utili*)

#70 (young people OR older people OR geriatric) AND (social care* OR social work*)

#71 #70 AND (research OR evidence)

#72 #71AND (use OR implement* OR appl* OR utili*)

#73 homeless* AND (social care* OR social work*)

#74 #73 AND (research OR evidence)

#75 #74 (use OR implement* OR appl* OR utili*)

#76 (mental ill* OR mental health) AND (social care* OR social work*)

#77 #76 AND (research OR evidence)

#78 #77 AND (use OR implement* OR appl* OR utili*)

#79 (substance use OR substance misuse) AND (social care* OR social work*)

#80 #79 AND (research OR evidence)

#81 #80 AND (use OR implement* OR appl* OR utili*)

#82 alcohol* AND (social care* OR social work*)

#83 #82 AND (research OR evidence)

#84 #83 AND (use OR implement* OR appl* OR utili*)

#85 child protection AND (social care* OR social work*)

#86 #85 AND (research OR evidence)

#87 #86 AND (use OR implement* OR appl* OR utili*)

#88 (respite OR foster OR domicil* OR residential OR day OR community) AND (care* OR service*)

#89 #88 AND (social care* OR social work*)

#90 #89 AND (research OR evidence)

#91 #90 AND (use OR implement* OR appl* OR utili*)

#92 (early years OR early intervention) AND (social care* OR social work*)

#93 #92 AND (research OR evidence)

#94 #93 AND (use OR implement* OR appl* OR utili*)

#95 community work*

#96 community work* and research

#97 #96 AND (use OR implement* OR appl* OR utili*)

#98 youth work*

#99 youth work* AND research

#100 nursery nurs*

****

AgeInfo

07/06/03

#1 evidence-based

#2 evidence-based practi*e

#3 best evidence

#4 research utili*

#5 research-based practi*e

#6 (research/evidence) based change

#7 evidence utili*

#8 research into practi*e

#9 evidence into practi*e

#10 best practi*e

#11 dissemin* AND best practi*e

#12 best practi*e AND (teaching and learning)

#13 evidence based AND (social care* OR social work*)

#14 what works

#15 knowledge based change

#16 model* AND learning

#17 model* AND research

#18 quality improvement*

#19 quality management

#20 quality assurance

#21 outcome research

#22 research impediment

#23 translat* AND research

#24 translat* AND finding*

#25 translat* AND result*

#26 effective AND practice*

#27 connect* AND (research and practice)

#28 adopt* AND (research and practice)

#29 practi*e focused

#30 research focused

#31 targeted dissemination

#32 targeted diffusion

#33 (appl* OR use OR implement* OR utili*) AND (research/evidence)

#34 evidence led

#35 research led

#36 learning culture

#37 model* AND management

#38 research minded*

#39 barrier* AND research

#40 human resource management

#41 criminal justice

#42 continuing professional development

#43 post qualifying education

#44 decision making AND research

#45 social work education

#46 organi* culture

#47 workplace learning

#48 innovation AND change

#49 diffusion AND innovation

#50 personnel management

#51 management AND evidence

#52 teaching method*

#53 constraint* AND research

#54 research AND access*

#55 research AND assimil*

#56 implement* AND strateg*

#57 knowledge AND transform*

#58 learning based change

#59 (learning disabl*/disabl*) AND (social care*/social work*)

#60 (abuse/neglect) AND (social care*/social work*)

#61 (young people/older people/geriatric) AND (social care*/social work*)

#62 homeless* AND (social care*/social work*)

#63 (mental ill*/mental health) AND (social care*/social work*)

#64 (substance use/substance misuse) AND (social care*/social work*)

#65 alcohol* AND (social care*/social work*)

#66 (respite/community/day/residential) AND (care* OR service*)

#67 #66 AND (social care*/social work*)

#68 community work*

#69 community work* AND research

#70 youth work*

****

Dissertation Abstracts (2002–2003)

24/06/03

#1 (evidence based)

#2 evidence PRE/1 based

#3 (evidence based practi?e)

#4 (research based practi?e)

#5 ((evidence OR research) based change)

#6 (research utili?)

#7 research PRE/1 utili?

#8 research w/1 utili?

#9 evidence w/1 utili?

#10 (best practi?e)

#11 (research into practi?e)

#12 (social care?) OR (social work?)

#13 (what works)

#14 #12 and research

#15 #12 and (research utili?)

#16 knowledge based change

#17 model? w/2 learning

#18 quality PRE/1 improvement?

#19 quality PRE/1 management

#20 quality PRE/1 assurance

#21 outcome w/1 research

#22 research w/2 impediment?

#23 translat? w/2 finding?

#24 translat? w/2 result?

#25 effective w/1 practi?

#26 connect? (research and practi?e)

#27 adopt? w/2 practi?e

#28 adopt w/2 evidence

#29 practi?e PRE/1 focus?

#30 research PRE/1 focus?

#31 targeted dissemination

#32 targeted diffusion

#33 diffusion PRE/2 evidence

#34 (research practi?e interaction)

#35 appl? PRE/2 research

#36 appl? PRE/2 evidence

#37 evidence led

#38 research led

#39 learning culture

#40 model? W/2 management

#41 research minded?

#42 barrier? W/2 research

#43 human resource management

#44 criminal justice

#45 continuing professional development

#46 post qualifying education

#47 workplace education

#48 decision making and research

#49 social work? Education

#50 organi?ational culture

#51 diffusion PRE/2 innovation?

#52 management and (evidence base?)

#53 teaching method?

#54 research access?

#55 research w/2 assimil?

#56 constraint? W/2 research

#57 knowledge w/2 transform?

#58 (learning disabl?) and ((social care?) OR (social work?))

#59 (abuse OR neglect) and ((social care?) OR (social work?))

#60 (elder? OR child? OR adolescent?) and ((social care?) OR (social work?))

#61 homeless? and ((social care?) OR (social work?))

#62 (mental ill? OR mental health) and ((social care?) OR (social work?))

#63 (substance use OR substance misuse) and ((social care?) OR (social work?))

#64 (child protection) and ((social care?) OR (social work?))

#65 (early years OR early intervention) and ((social care?) OR (social work?))

#66 youth work?

#67 community work?

#68 nursery nurs?

****

ChildData

09/07/03

#1 evidence based

#2 evidence based practice

#3 best evidence based

#4 research utili*

#5 research based practice*

#6 research based practice*

#7 (research OR evidence) based change

#8 evidence AND utili*

#9 research into practice

#10 evidence into practice

#11 best practice

#12 best practice AND (teaching and learning)

#13 evidence based (social care* OR social work*)

#14 what works

#15 knowledge based change

#16 model* of learning

#17 model* AND research utili*

#18 quality improvement*

#19 quality management

#20 quality assurance

#21 outcome research

#22 research impediment

#23 translat* AND finding*

#24 translat* AND result*

#25 translat* AND research

#26 effective practice*

#27 connect* AND (research and practice)

#28 adopt* AND (research and practice)

#29 practice focused

#30 research focused

#31 targeted dissemination

#32 targeted diffusion

#33 research practice interaction

#34 appl* of (research OR evidence)

#35 implement* of (research OR evidence)

#36 use of (research OR evidence)

#37 evidence led

#38 learning culture

#39 research led

#40 model* AND management

#41 research minded*

#42 barrier* to research AND (social care* OR social work*)

#43 human resource management

#44 criminal justice AND (social care* OR social work*)

#45 continuing professional development

#46 post qualifying education

#47 decision making AND research

#48 social work education

#49 organi?atinal culture

#50 workplace learning

#51 innovation AND change

#52 diffusion AND innovation

#53 personnel management

#54 management AND evidence based

#55 teaching method*

#56 constraint* AND research

#57 research access*

#58 research assimil*

#59 implement* strateg*

#60 knowledge transfer

#61 learning based change

#62 diploma OR degree OR NVQ OR national vocational qualification

#63 learning disabl* OR disabl*

#64 #63 AND (research OR evidence)

#65 #64 AND (utili* OR use OR implement* OR appl*)

#66 abuse OR neglect

#67 #66 AND (research OR evidence)

#68 #67 AND (utili* OR use OR implement* OR appl*)

#69 young people OR older people OR geriatric

#70 #69 AND (research OR evidence)

#71 #70 AND (utili* OR use OR implement* OR appl*)

#72 homeless*

#73 #72 AND (research OR evidence)

#74 #73 AND (utili* OR use OR implement* OR appl*)

#75 mental ill* OR mental health

#76 #75 AND (research OR evidence)

#77 AND (utili* OR use OR implement* OR appl*)

#78 substance use OR substance misuse

#79 #78 AND (research OR evidence)

#80 #79 AND (utili* OR use OR implement* OR appl*)

#81 acohol*

#82 #81 AND (research OR evidence)

#83 #82 AND (utili* OR use OR implement* OR appl*)

#84 child protection

#85 #84 AND (research OR evidence)

#86 #85 AND (utili* OR use OR implement* OR appl*)

#87 respite OR foster OR domicil* OR day OR community

#88 #87 AND (care* OR service*)

#89 #88 AND (research OR evidence)

#90 #89 AND (utili* OR use OR implement* OR appl*)

#91 early years OR early intervention

#92 #91 AND (research OR evidence)

#93 #92 AND (utili* OR use OR implement* OR appl*)

#94 youth work*

#95 #94 AND (research OR evidence)

#96 community work*

#97 #96 AND (research OR evidence)

#98 nursery nurs*

#99 #98 AND (research OR evidence)

Website searches
12/05/03

Society for Social Work and Research
www.sswr.org

National Association of Social Workers
www.naswdc.org

Centre for Evidence-based Social Services
www.ex.ac.uk/cebss

International Federation of Social Workers
www.ifsw.org

Hadley Centre for Adoption and Foster Care Studies
http://www.bris.ac.uk/sps/research/fpcw/hadley/default.shtml

Nordic Campbell Center
http://www.sfi.dk/sw1270.asp

Australian Association of Social Workers
www.aasw.asn.au

Australasian Cochrane Centre
http://www.cochrane.org.au/

Canadian Association of Social Workers
www.casw-acts.ca

Barnardo's
www.barnardos.org

Research in Practice
www.rip.org.uk

Making Research Count
www.uea.ac.uk/swk/research/mrc/welcome.htm

Joseph Rowntree Foundation
www.jrf.org.uk

Economic and Social Research Council
www.esrc.ac.uk

Regard
www.regard.ac.uk

Care and Health
www.careandhealth.com

Social Care Association
www.socialcaring.co.uk

Social Work Access Network
www.sc.edu/swan

Council on Social Work Education
www.cswe.org

Information for Practice
http://www.nyu.edu/socialwork/wwwrsw/ip/

Index

Other knowledge reviews available from SCIE

KNOWLEDGE REVIEW 1
Learning and teaching in social work education: Assessment
Beth R. Crisp, Mark R. Anderson, Joan Orme and Pam Green Lister
1 904812 00 7
November 2003

KNOWLEDGE REVIEW 2
The adoption of looked after children: A scoping review of research
Alan Rushton
1 904812 01 5
November 2003

KNOWLEDGE REVIEW 3
Types and quality of knowledge in social care
Ray Pawson, Annette Boaz, Lesley Grayson, Andrew Long and Colin Barnes
1 904812 02 3
November 2003

KNOWLEDGE REVIEW 4
Innovative, tried and tested: A review of good practice in fostering
Clive Sellick and Darren Howell
1 904812 03 1
November 2003

KNOWLEDGE REVIEW 5
Fostering success: An exploration of the research literature in foster care
Kate Wilson, Ian Sinclair, Claire Taylor, Andrew Pithouse and Clive Sellick
1 904812 04 X
January 2004

KNOWLEDGE REVIEW 6
Teaching and learning communication skills in social work education
Pamela Trevithick, Sally Richards, Gillian Ruch and Bernard Moss
with Linda Lines and Oded Manor
1 904812 12 0
May 2004